MAKE WAY FOR THE GRAND ILLUSIONIST

Poetry by Callie Miller
Photography by Missy Miller

PEAK & PINE PRESS
Denver, Colorado

This collection of poems and photographs represents the creative expression of the author and photographer. While inspired by personal reflection, the works are not intended as literal depictions of specific people, places, or events. Any resemblance to actual persons, living or dead, or to real events or locales, is purely coincidental.

Library of Congress Control Number: 2025919984
ISBN: 979-8-9998714-1-1

Printed in the United States of America.

Photography and book design by Missy Miller of Moments by Missy LLC.

CONTENTS

Left to themselves people grow their hair.
Left to themselves they take off their shoes.

-Diane di Prima

MAKE WAY FOR THE GRAND ILLUSIONIST

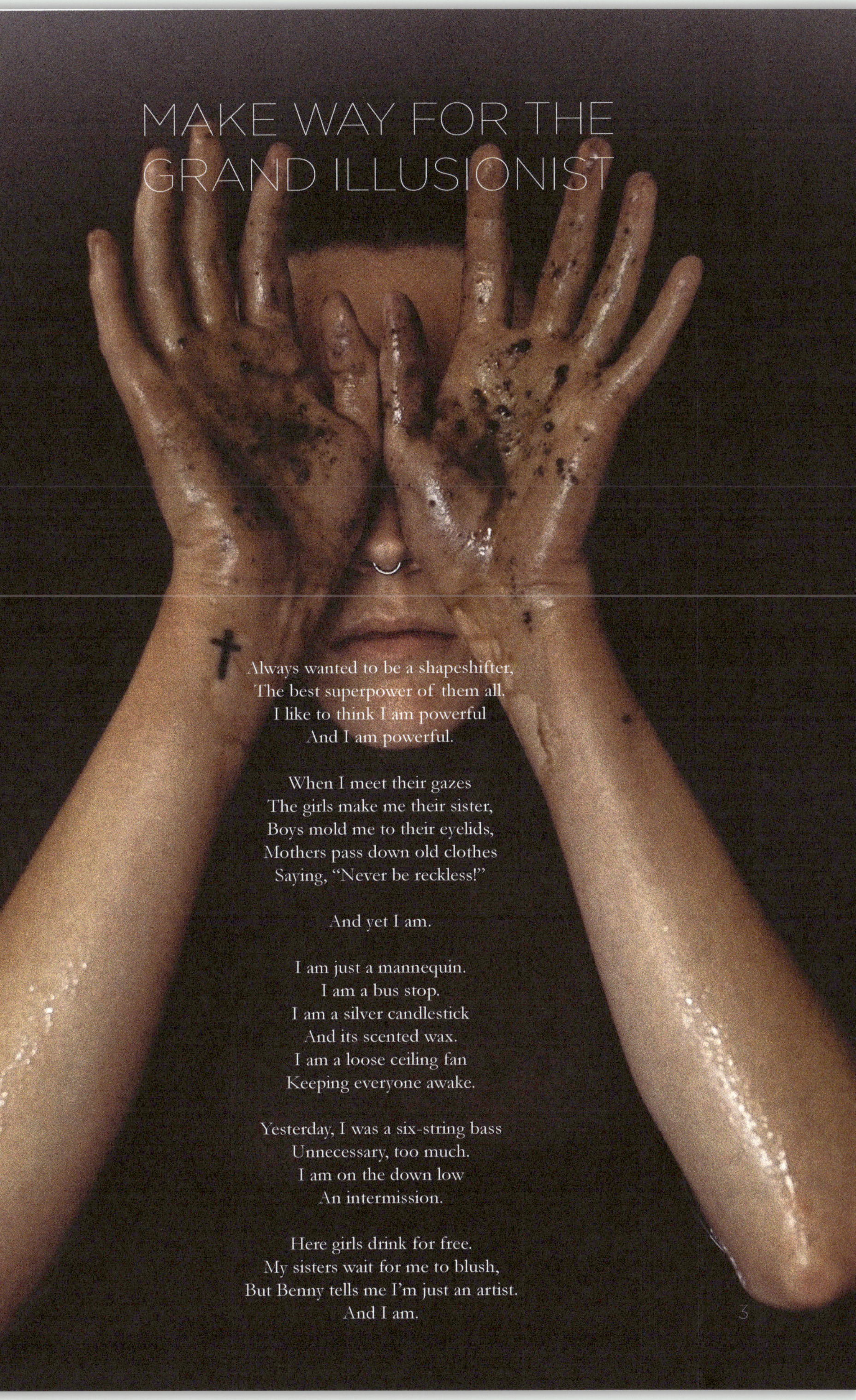

Always wanted to be a shapeshifter,
The best superpower of them all.
I like to think I am powerful
And I am powerful.

When I meet their gazes
The girls make me their sister,
Boys mold me to their eyelids,
Mothers pass down old clothes
Saying, "Never be reckless!"

And yet I am.

I am just a mannequin.
I am a bus stop.
I am a silver candlestick
And its scented wax.
I am a loose ceiling fan
Keeping everyone awake.

Yesterday, I was a six-string bass
Unnecessary, too much.
I am on the down low
An intermission.

Here girls drink for free.
My sisters wait for me to blush,
But Benny tells me I'm just an artist.
And I am.

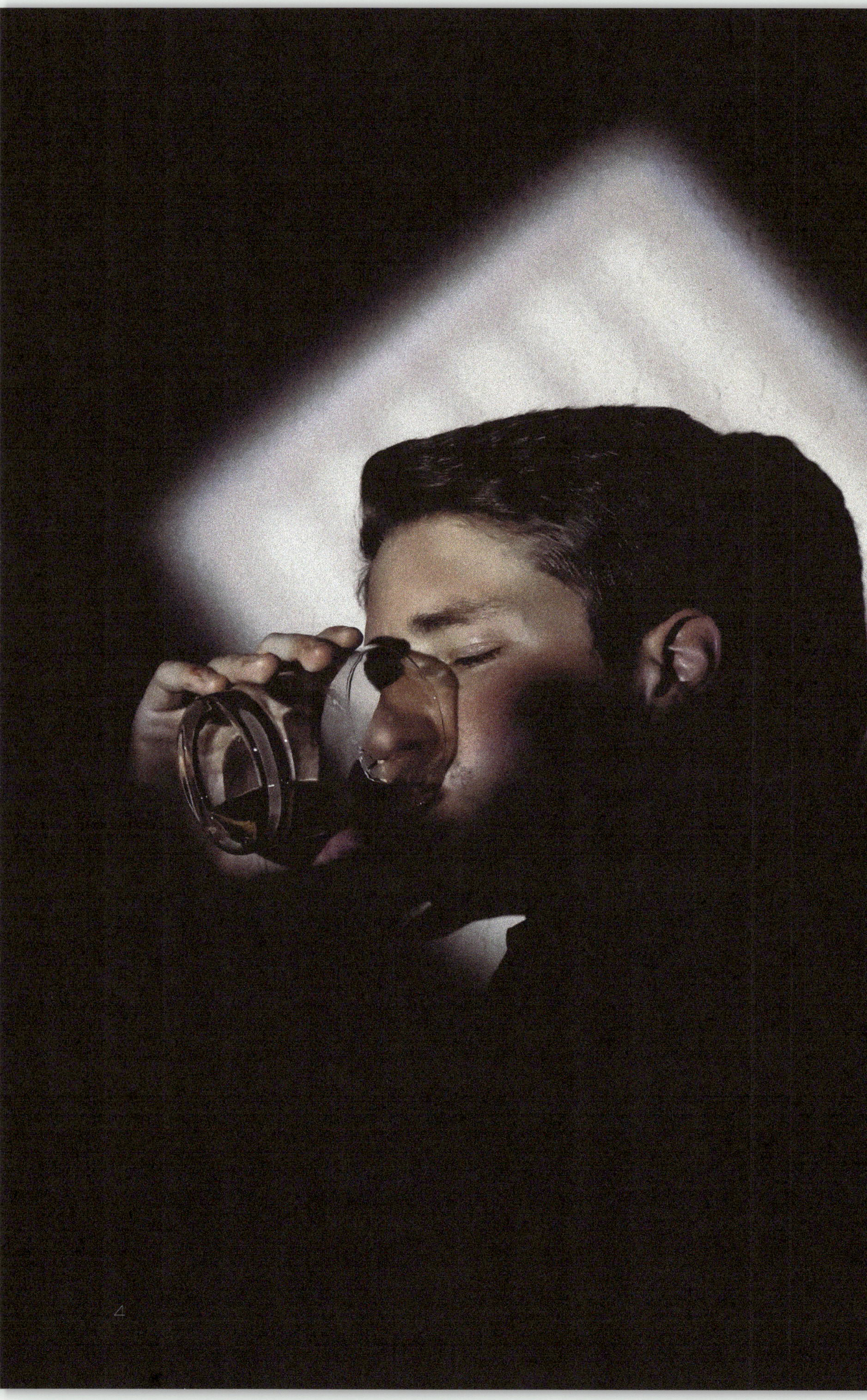

CUL-DE-SAC

When you took me in I asked for your name.
"Two cocktails and one olive," you said
"Share it between the two."
The two of us? No, the cocktails.
After that you tied a knot
With the back of your hand but
Your tongue stayed silent all night.

Dream of me driving, Mercedes-man.
Don't think of what to call me,
Call me a catch,
Call me a Rolex, a mint leaf, a portrait of your mother.
Stretch your hand to my cheek,
Scratch your palm, and let the alcohol burn
In the shallow cuts and hangnails
While I drive in circles.

To park gently is not to stop.
On rainy nights, lightning bolts through
Garage windows are like gunshots,
And my ears are still ringing
From the storm last week.

The bar, the car, the garage,
It all becomes the same
Without names, and gasoline
Tanks mean nothing to me.

IMPRESSION

I wanted you to see the black-slippered
Silk-vest cat-eyed
Skin-tight woman.
Wanted you to see the soft
Silhouette I leave,
Crumpled sheets,
And how late I come home.

What time of day
Did you realize I was a lie?
The blue-washed turtleneck
High-waisted sweatpants
Of a soil soul,
Succulent, herb garden girl,
Parched of sunlight.

Was it that first Saturday night
At a sticky 11:04 pm when,
Knowing all along how
My laugh sounded
And feet tripped,
You knew I'd eat up
Your compliments?

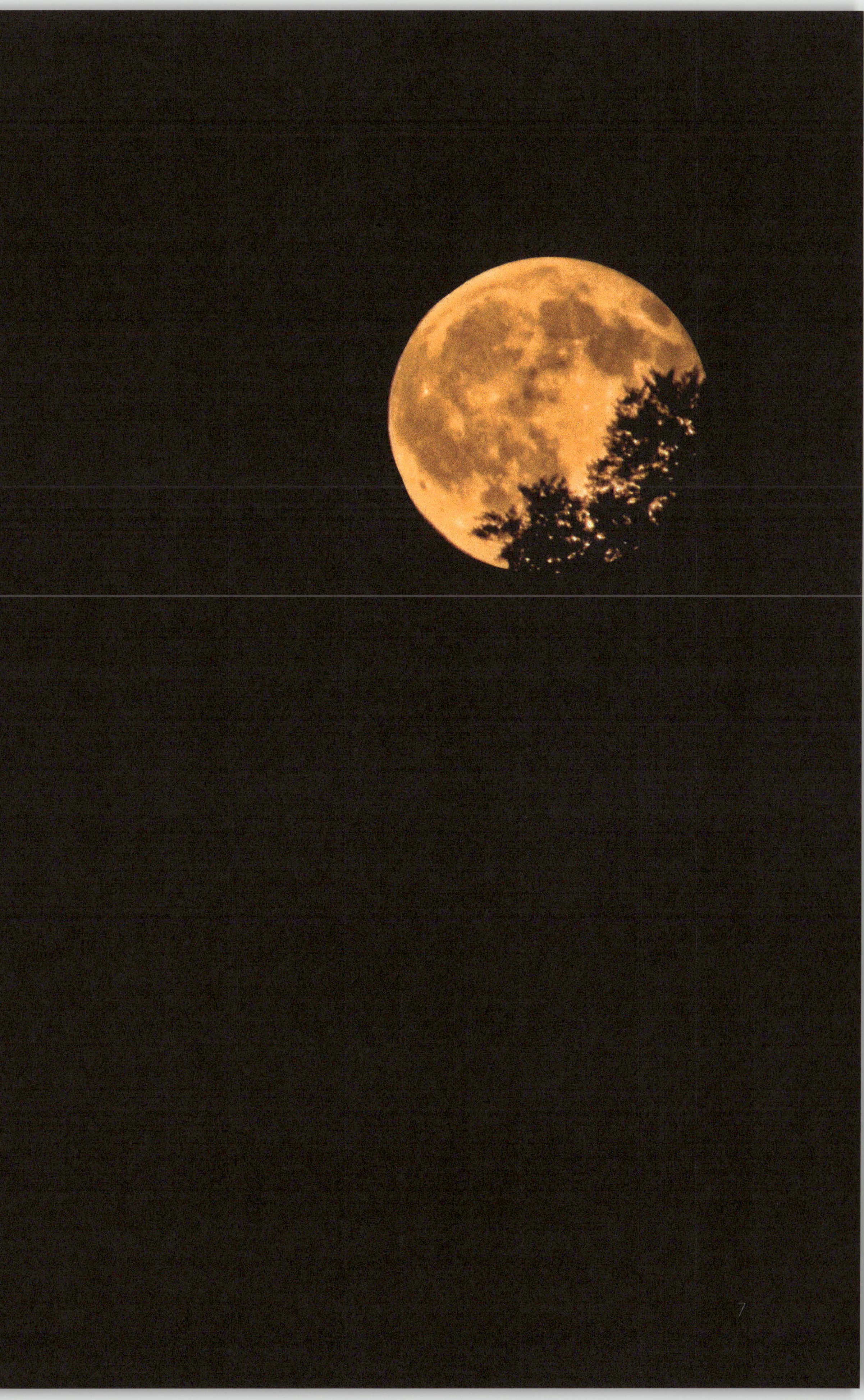

LOCKED DOWN

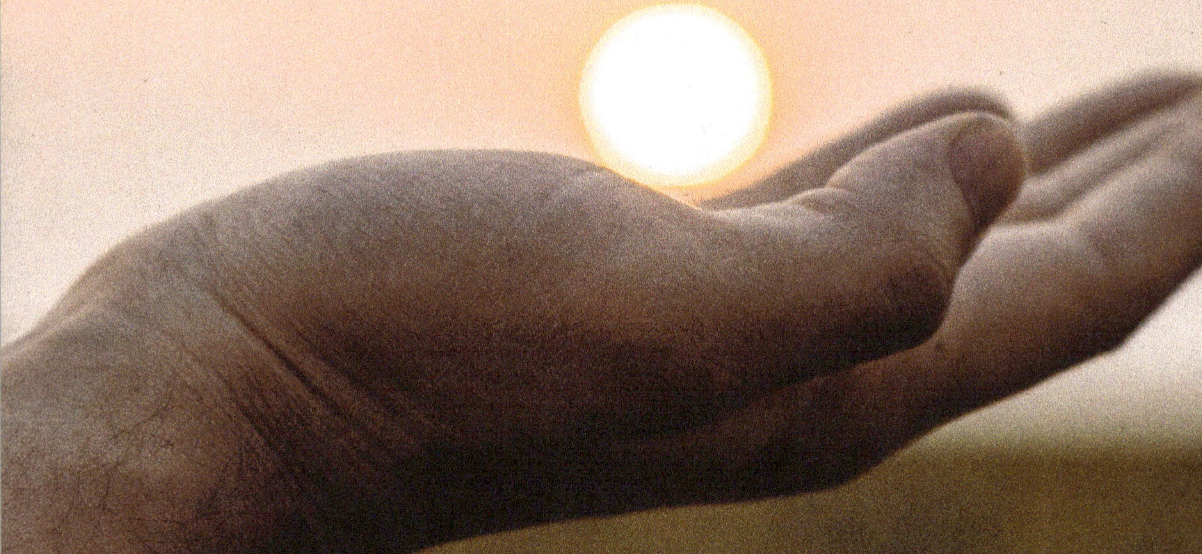

You speak to me in hushed tones,
A soft touch, as if starved.
We are isolated in this house spine
(Three stories, two characters)
Where the lights don't turn themselves off
And we still don't know how the switch works.

My favorite pictures become bleached next to my window.
A blue cheesecloth, a lemon, and faraway postcards;
We watch them while the sun sets,
Now muted, like palms over ears.

We keep awake with an elevator chime
In the orange of daytime, orange of dark.
Don't listen. Keep your hands still.
Just wait it out.

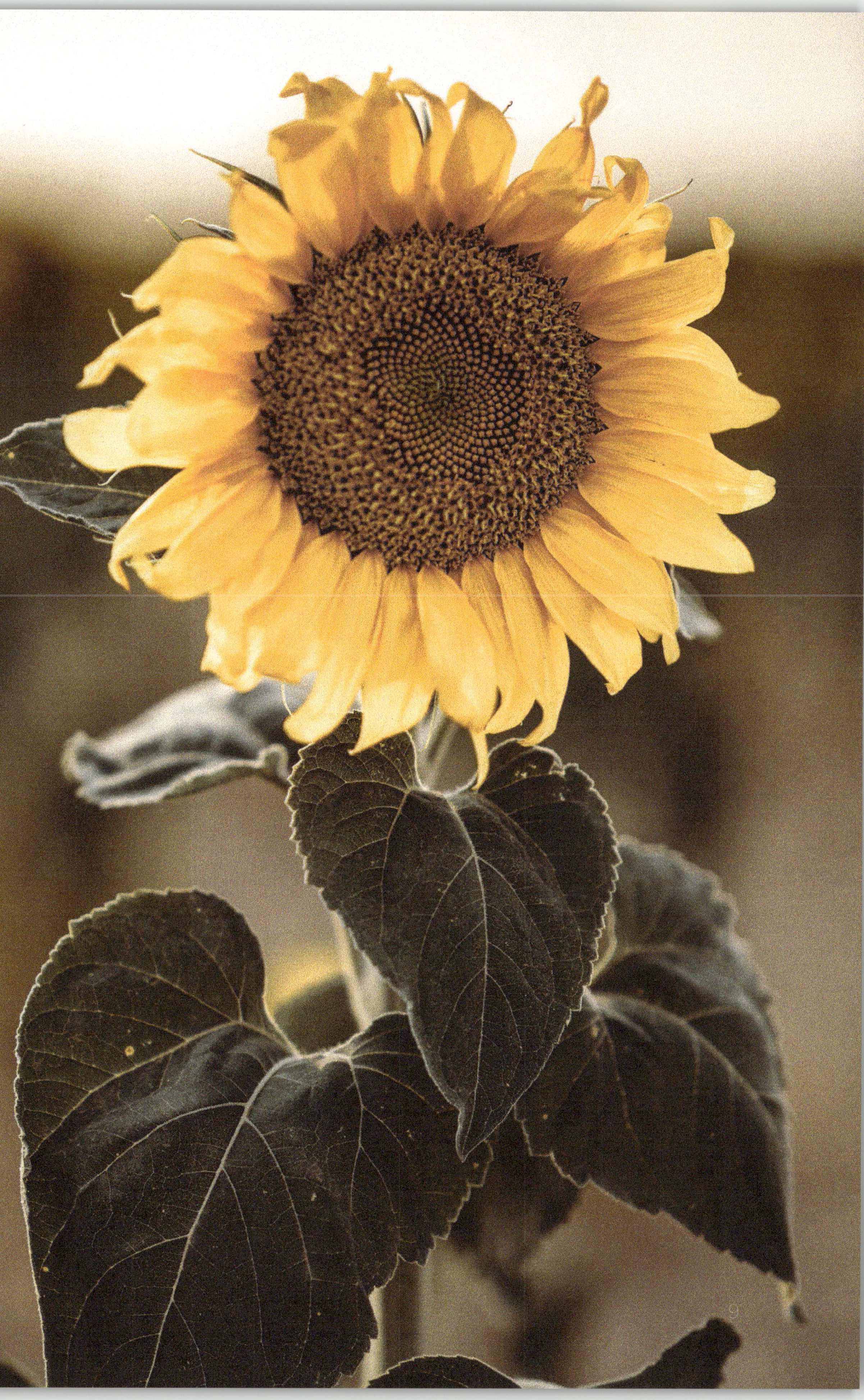

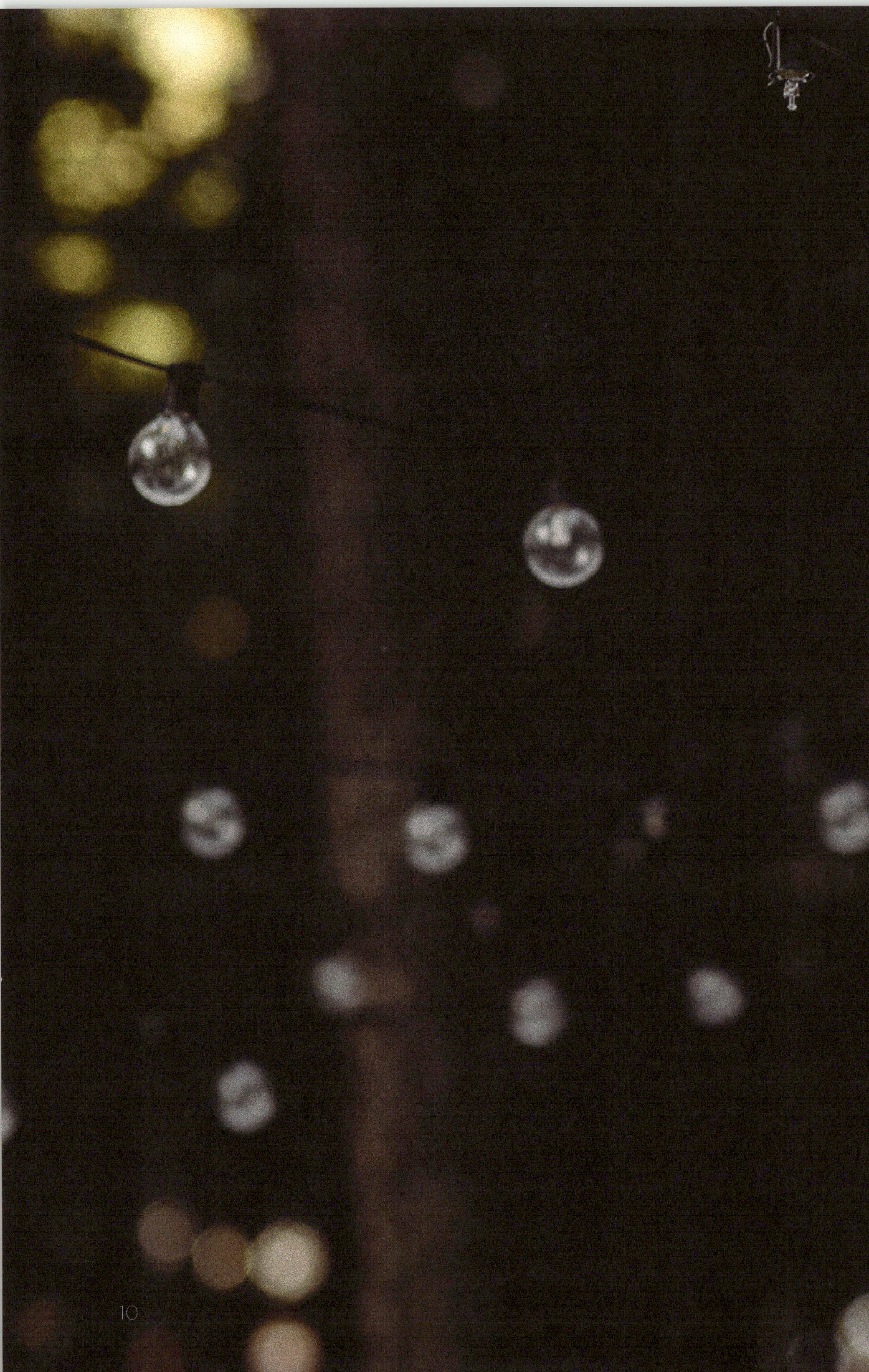

BUSY BABY

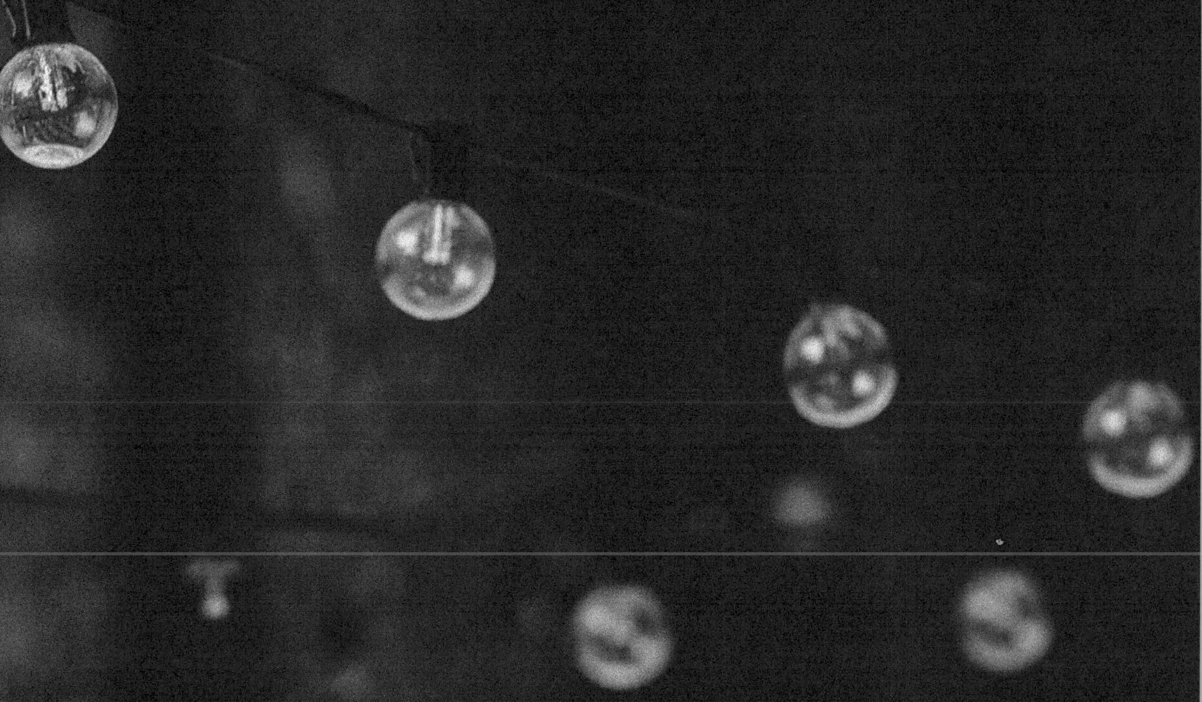

O'Hara's words linger above my head,
I do not like Coke.

Just smell my hair,
Take me to museums,
I'll write string lights for you.

Don't leave the sliding door open
In fear of a summer chill,
Hearing a dog cry,
Red sirens,
You leaving.

I'll keep busy, baby,
Taping poems on my walls,
Bribes on my windows,
They face south.
I turn my back and the sun leaves.

DAY 3

I'm told I must withdraw from you now.
The sun rises each morning and
Curtains don't keep it out anymore

Waking up early helps me
Keep my plants alive
There is nothing to see here

I hear birds chirping over rooftops
Another day to stay clean
I've scrubbed my bathtub 3 times today

This is day 3
I'd like to get drunk with you
Anything but clean

I remember you packing
Starting and ending packing
Our 3-second hug goodbye

I've become a potted spruce
I'm a grandfather minute-hand
I am only tunnel vision

You are gone & I do this all by myself.

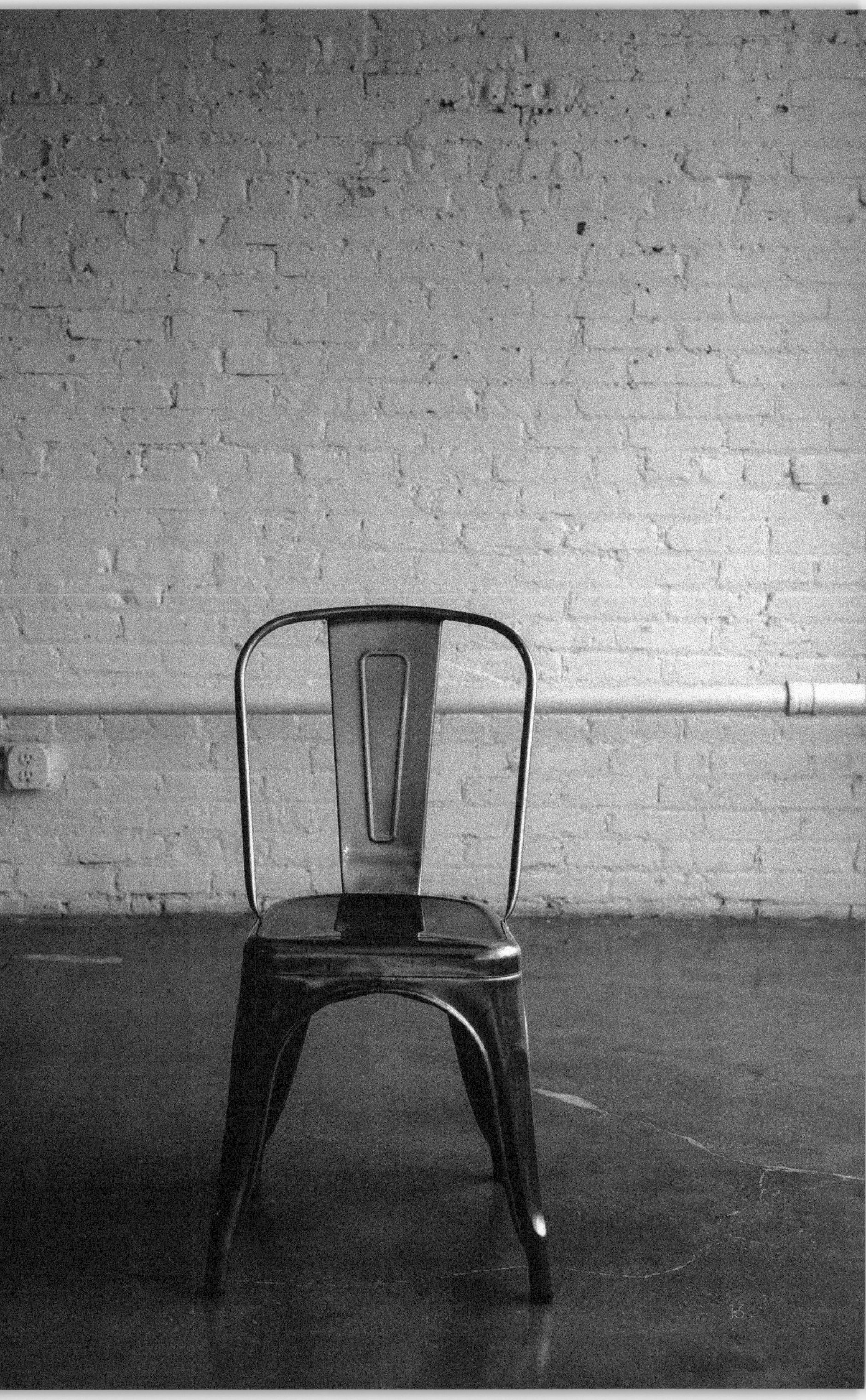

II

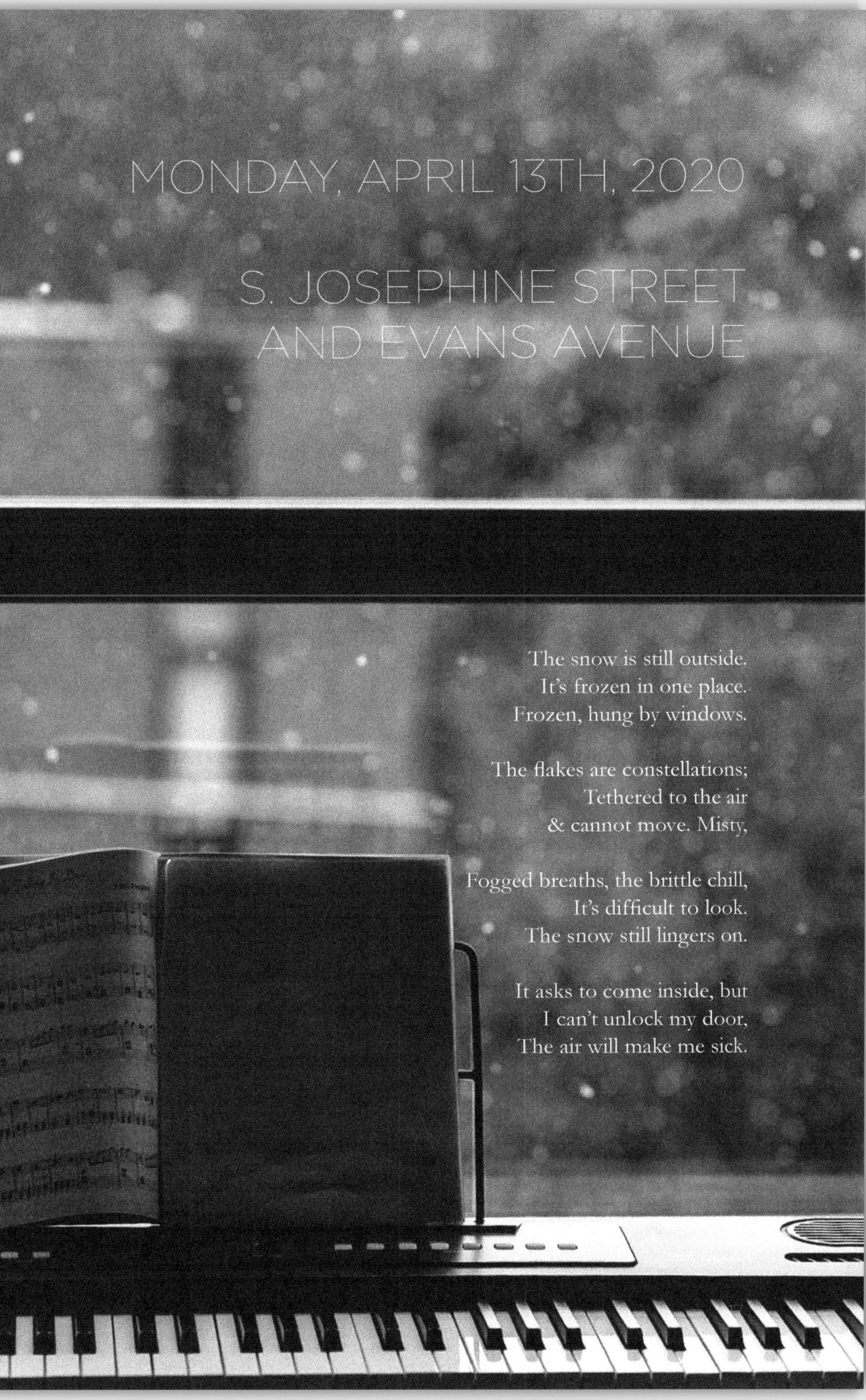

MONDAY, APRIL 13TH, 2020

S. JOSEPHINE STREET AND EVANS AVENUE

The snow is still outside.
It's frozen in one place.
Frozen, hung by windows.

The flakes are constellations;
Tethered to the air
& cannot move. Misty,

Fogged breaths, the brittle chill,
It's difficult to look.
The snow still lingers on.

It asks to come inside, but
I can't unlock my door,
The air will make me sick.

PHLOX MOON

The neighbors never see me.
Their hazy lungs
Scream throughout the day.
Their bass breaks, trapped inside,
And I scream with them.

I pick flowers by the road to
Dry them out in jelly jars.
I'm sick of untangling bike chains,
Stuck at the bottom of a hill
I ride in circles.
Return. Bathe.

Denver air but it's dark
And pink under the moon,
A full glow.
Wake me up,
Take me outside,
Howl with me.
Listen for my friends.

MADE UP

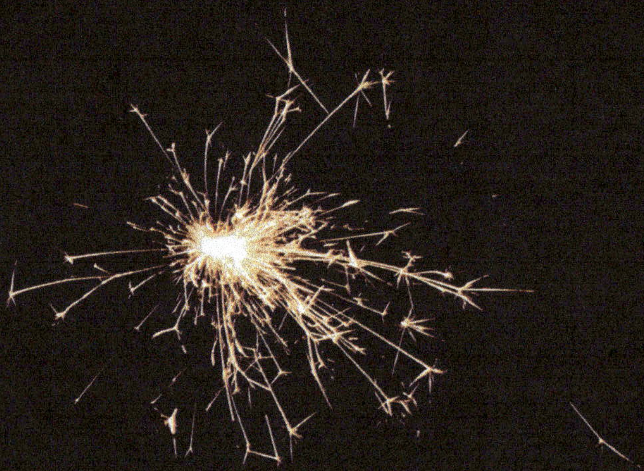

Do your cheeks rouge in the mirror too?
It's like a bitter, booze glow.
I decide to make myself up,
I've become a tired expression
In this white light of winter,
In this old bedroom
Every day.

Upper lid glitter glue
And lips and lips and cheeks.
I am a highlighter woman,
And I am only tonight.

But now I am the morning dew,
Now I am the shimmer and disco ball glory
That runs past my chin, into my cleavage.
Smell sweat and day-old shampoo,
I am no longer glossed.
I am spiked. Glass shards of eye-rolling
And REM sleep deprivation.
I grind this sand in my teeth
To exfoliate my gums. Pulp.

Glitter blush and residue
Pool at the jugular,
The supraclavicular, suprasternal,
Scientific for too boney,
And I am left with only the mirror.

UNNATURAL

Next to my window are seven tall stalks of a forget-me-not, the same forget-me-not that grew from seedlings in a paper packet. The left two stems are leaning far over the plastic container they're planted in, but the rest are standing straight up. The remaining leaves are getting sunburnt but they didn't do that in the past, it must be getting unbearably sunny and hot. All the tiny, blue flower blooms like leaning on the glass of the window, as if they're looking out into the fresh air. Or like they want to escape. It's beyond me, but I do understand their wishes. When the petals fall off the flowers, they'll stick to the window and turn it to stained glass when the sun shines through the blue. Some of the stems are dying off, I can already see them withering, but it's hard for me to give up on them. These flowers remain so different from the other pots I have outside, there must be something about indoor air and filtered sunlight. Each stem is so spindly and long, pale and maybe sickly. Like a weed, they keep growing taller and want to wrap around my walls. I should prune the stems back, take out the dying ones, and see if it will outlast the autumn.

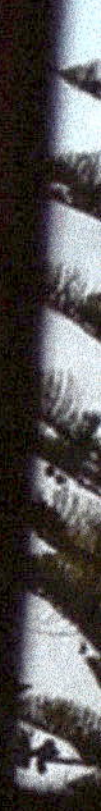

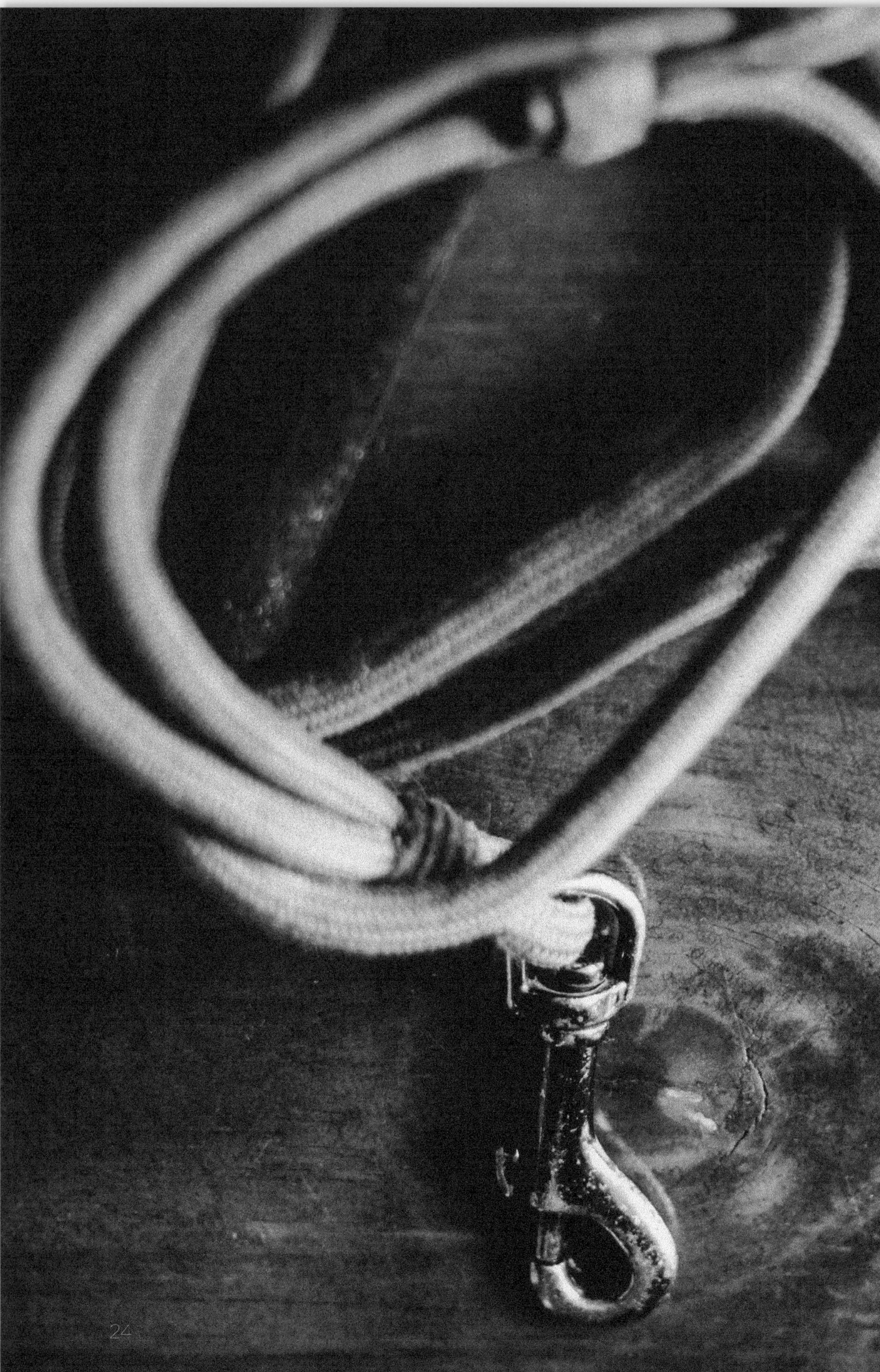

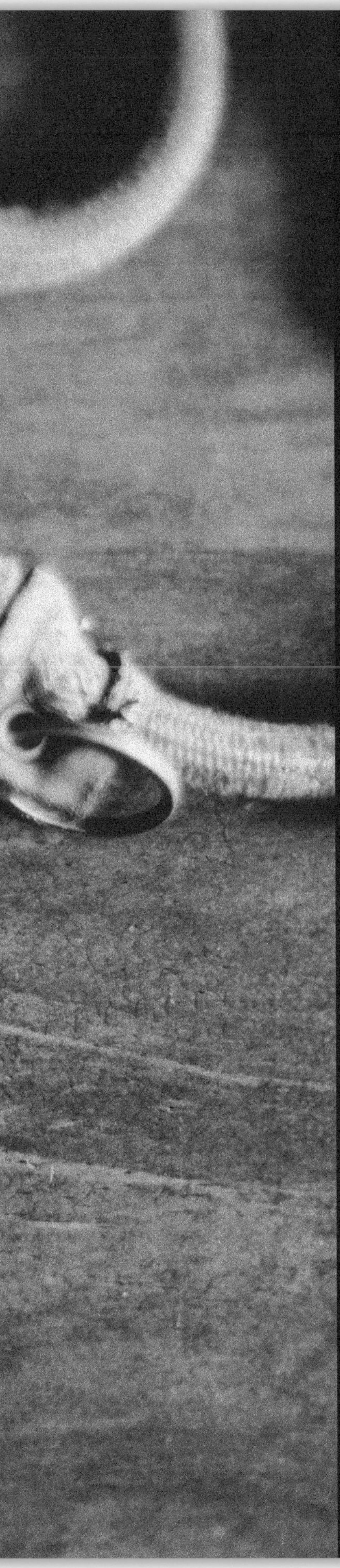

KALANCHOE TOMENTOSA

When you died, I bought a plant
From the worn-down Lowe's
Cactus and succulent section.
I bought a new pot, some soil.
I named him Teddy.

I brought Teddy home,
Put him on a windowsill
Three feet from my bed,
And left him on a candle lid
To catch the spill.

By southern windows, he adapts
As a sunshine lover.
He soaks in radiance.
You loved the sunshine too,
Always bathing.

Soft touch and sweet best friend,
He holds my hand in the morning,
Only listens when I breathe,
I almost named him Grief.

When Teddy wilts, I water him,
Splashing onto the window pane.
You comforted my sadness,
Begged me to come home,
But Teddy can't even tell me to stay put.

Teddy, with an extra arm,
Has lived with me a month now,
And I wonder if he'll live forever.

SOMETHING'S MISSING

When you wake up standing over the railing
Just outside of room 301
Your feet were taking you to Mother's bedside
But the walls rejected your flesh memory.

I am trying to be here
Where nothing is placed where it is in my mind.
Three types of milk should be in the refrigerator
Two flights of stairs, new hardwood floors
Eight pairs of shoes; everyone needs at least two under the bench
A bath drain of dog hair
Porch lights left on overnight.

All I have is a week's worth of clothing
And half-used soap bottles.
The milk's gone sour.

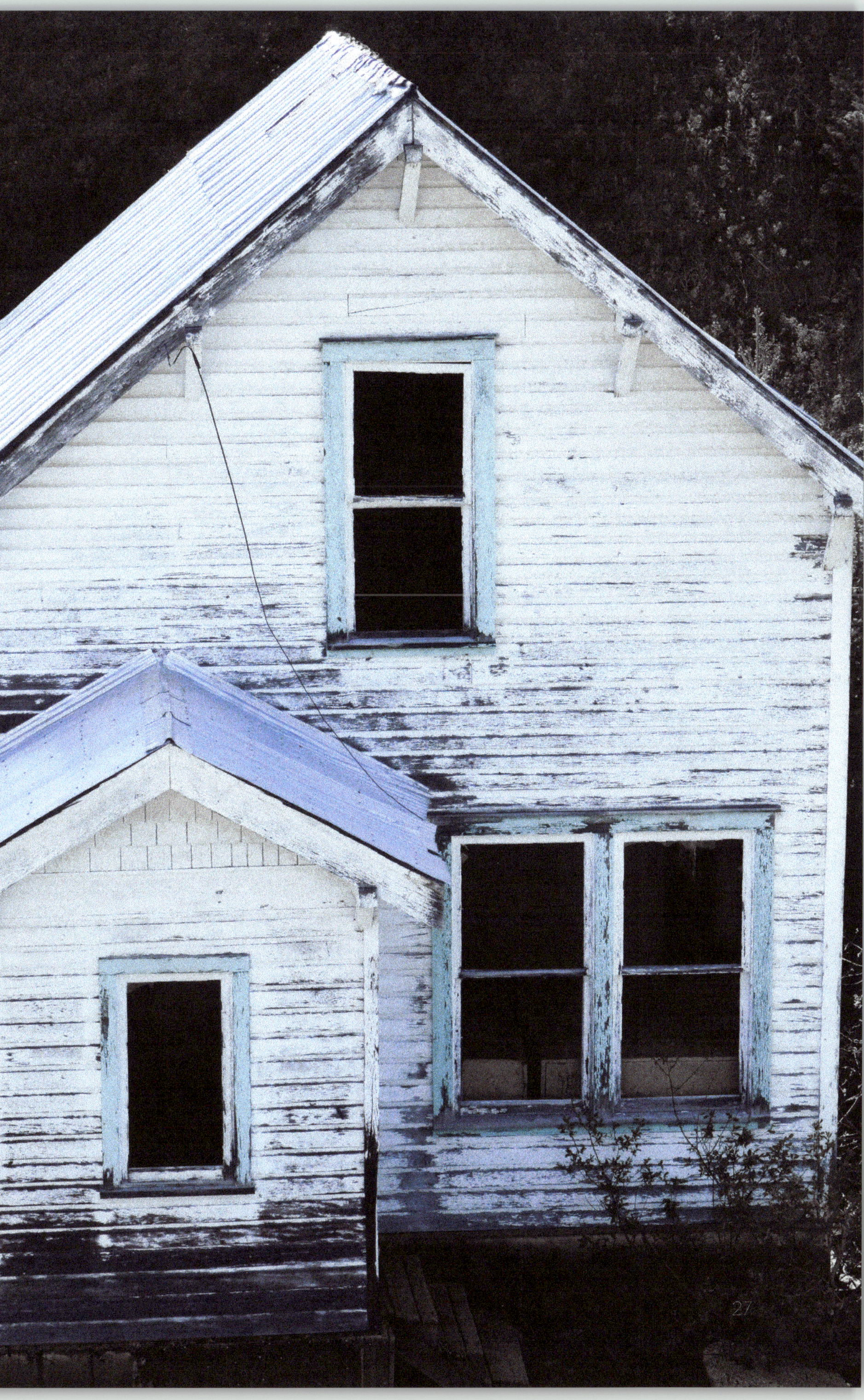

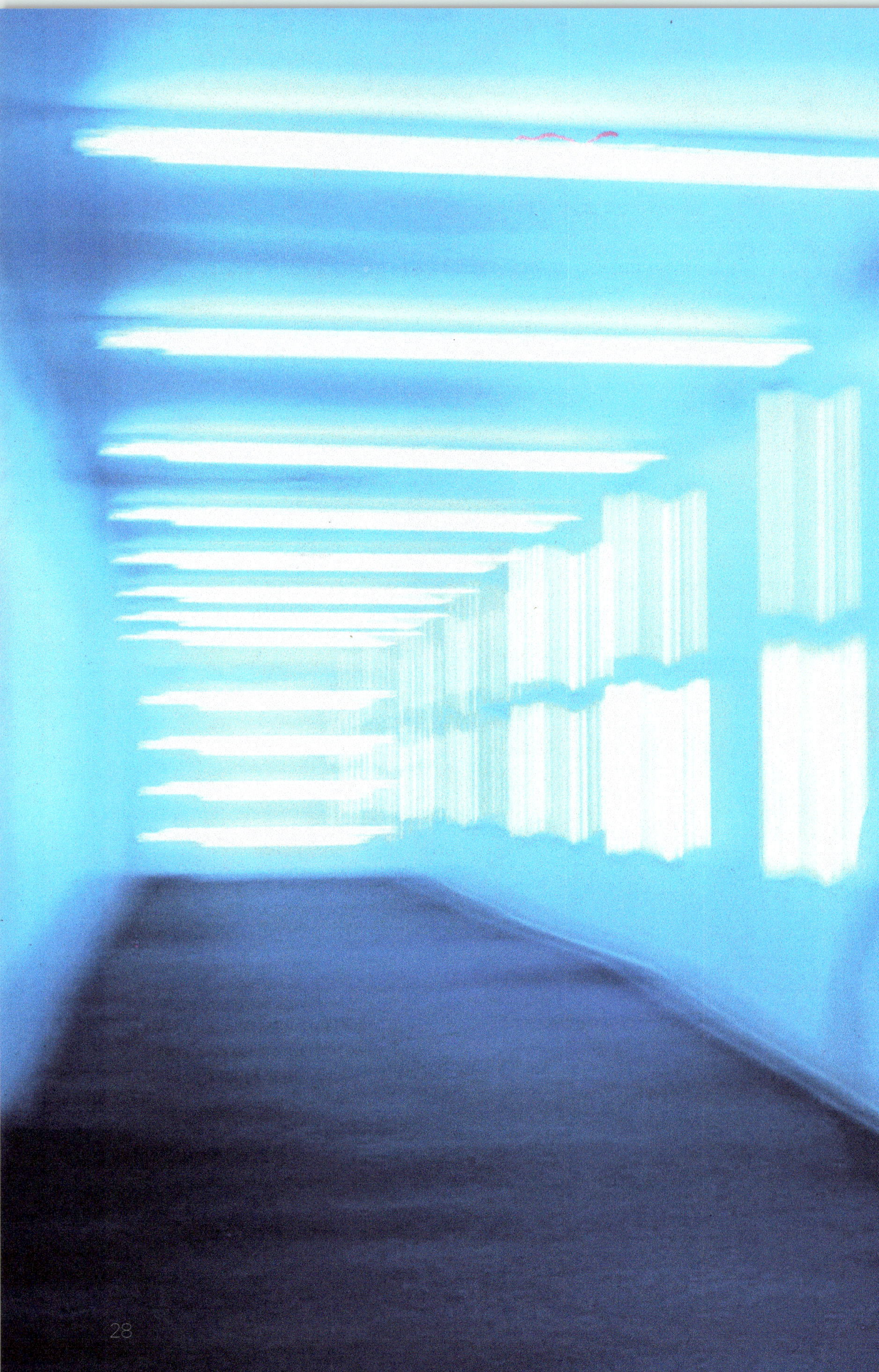

MY FRIEND

Steven lives in a studio apartment.
The vibrant red brick and black floor tiles
Make him look taller, stand straighter
And the rooftop terrace means a place
For sun salutations
And his neighbors always offer leftover desserts.

On his worst days, Steven will cook three meals and
Watch Netflix until the next Tinder match or
Weekly family Facetime, and even then,
He will only stay on the phone for an hour.

He'll keep to himself now that his roommate moved out
And he can't even find a leftover King Soopers receipt
At the bottom of his reusable grocery bags and
It's been two weeks, so his sheets are clean again and
He's onto a new bar of soap from the farmer's market with
Money left to buy the next carton of oat milk and
At least the dentist still calls every six months,
At least the dentist still calls him every six months,
At least the dentist still calls me every six months.

PARCHED

Forget disease and think forest
Think of light refracting pink through the belly
Of a pitcher plant.
Or green mouths and teeth to rake the air.

I want a carnivorous plant
To purr its own life into my lifeless air.
I can feed it as my own child,
Reminding myself to eat while I'm at it

I doubt the flowers on my windowsill
Know we are hurting outside.
All they've known is soil
Recycled pots and
Filtered water from my bathroom faucet.

My forget-me-nots forgot
The word "pandemic."
I keep my windows shut.

My daisies stopped growing in this sickness,
This sick is my own foul air.
I still find dead flies in the windowsill.

I want a carnivorous plant
To clean up the fat flies
Fruit flies
Sweaty air
And night terrors

Flies buzz too much at night,
They never go to use
And I am here with them
Pawing, clawing
At the dirt and the muck.
They're sick, unwell,
Think carcass,
My plants turn to carcass
1 every 12 days,

I'm saying I want something
To hunger for my own health.

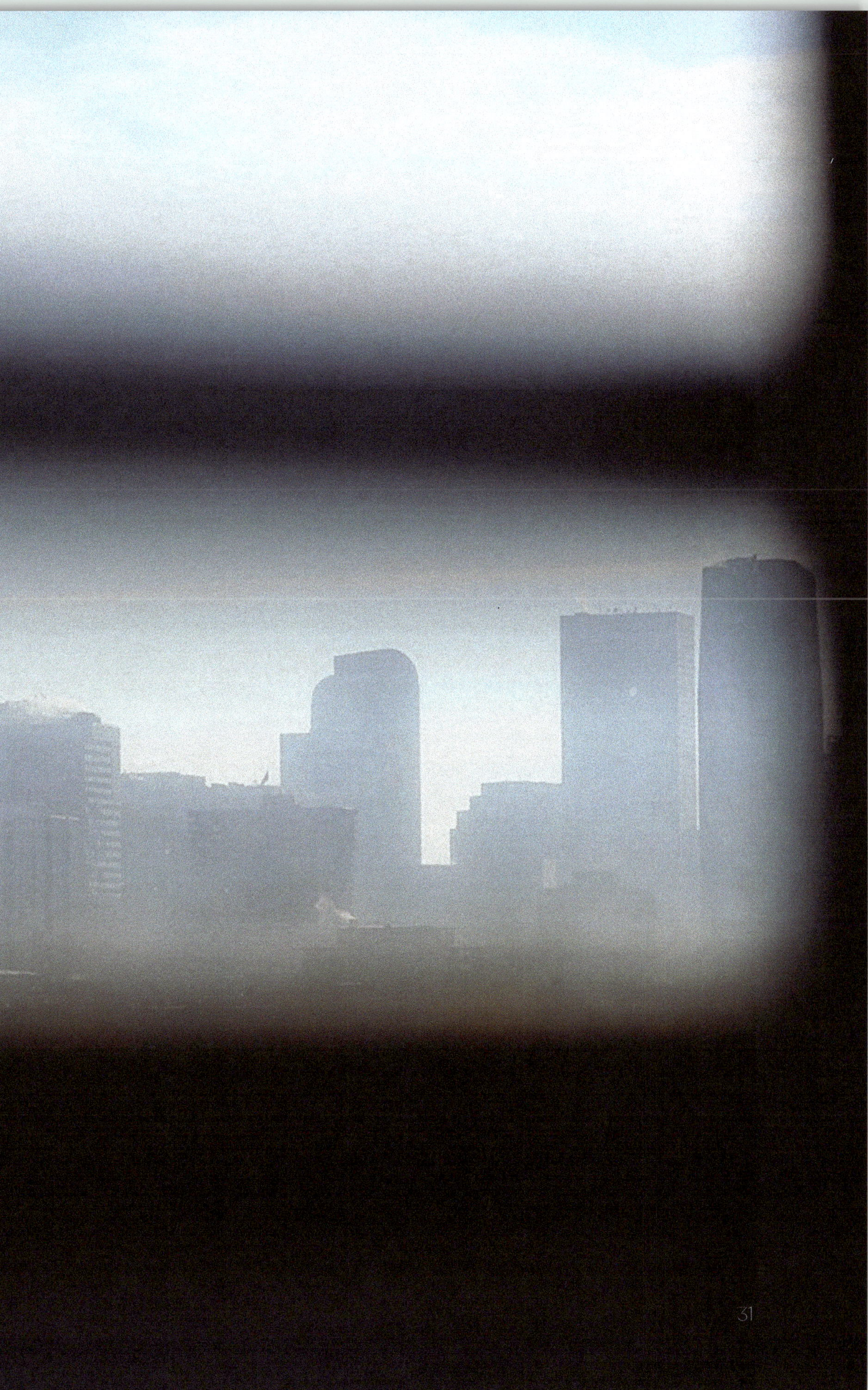

STREWN

There are purple feathers scattered about the floor, intertwining,
Tangling the carpet fibers, and I trample them on my way
To wash, refresh.
The dishes are piling up in the sink,
On my nightstands, on the small coffee table.
I forgot to wash my face three nights in a row, and I'm on my
Last roll of toilet paper, last box of tissues.

My eyes beg me for a new prescription and I have six missed calls
From my doctor. Ground beef, black beans, and chopped tomatoes
Become putrid in the refrigerator as my roommates neglect my shelf.
It's two steps to the garbage, but I'm stuck picking the feathers out of my socks,
Out of my slip-on dresses, out of the shower drain.

There are spoonfuls of soil in my bathtub
And an unopened bottle of aromatherapy bubble soap
Meant for people who enjoy warm baths.
My bag of Miracle-Gro sprouts new mold
Every month and the smell of white, fuzzy earth
Lingers through my bedroom for two days.
I let it air out for a week.

I know that when I plug my ears it sounds like an earthquake,
Maybe the rumble of an underground train.
I also know that filling my ears with water
Sounds like a hearty windstorm,
Or how I'd assume drowning sounds
I think the candle I lit last night has drowned itself,
And last week's fruit flies will dive-bomb the wax
Before crusting over.

Nothing quite sounds like sleeping,
But my mouth will hang open
In bed tonight
On an empty stomach,
Hoping tomorrow I will avoid the feathers.

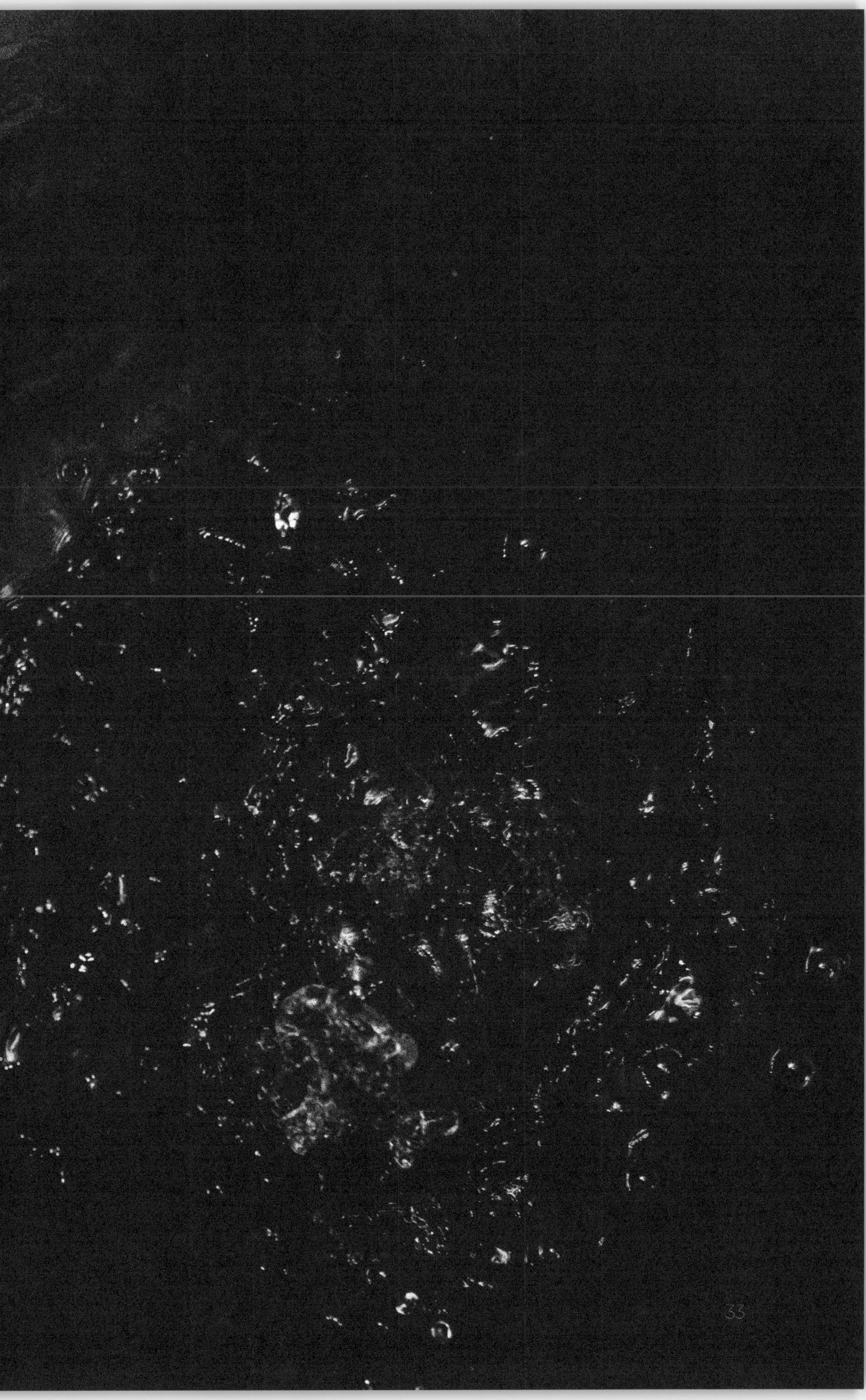

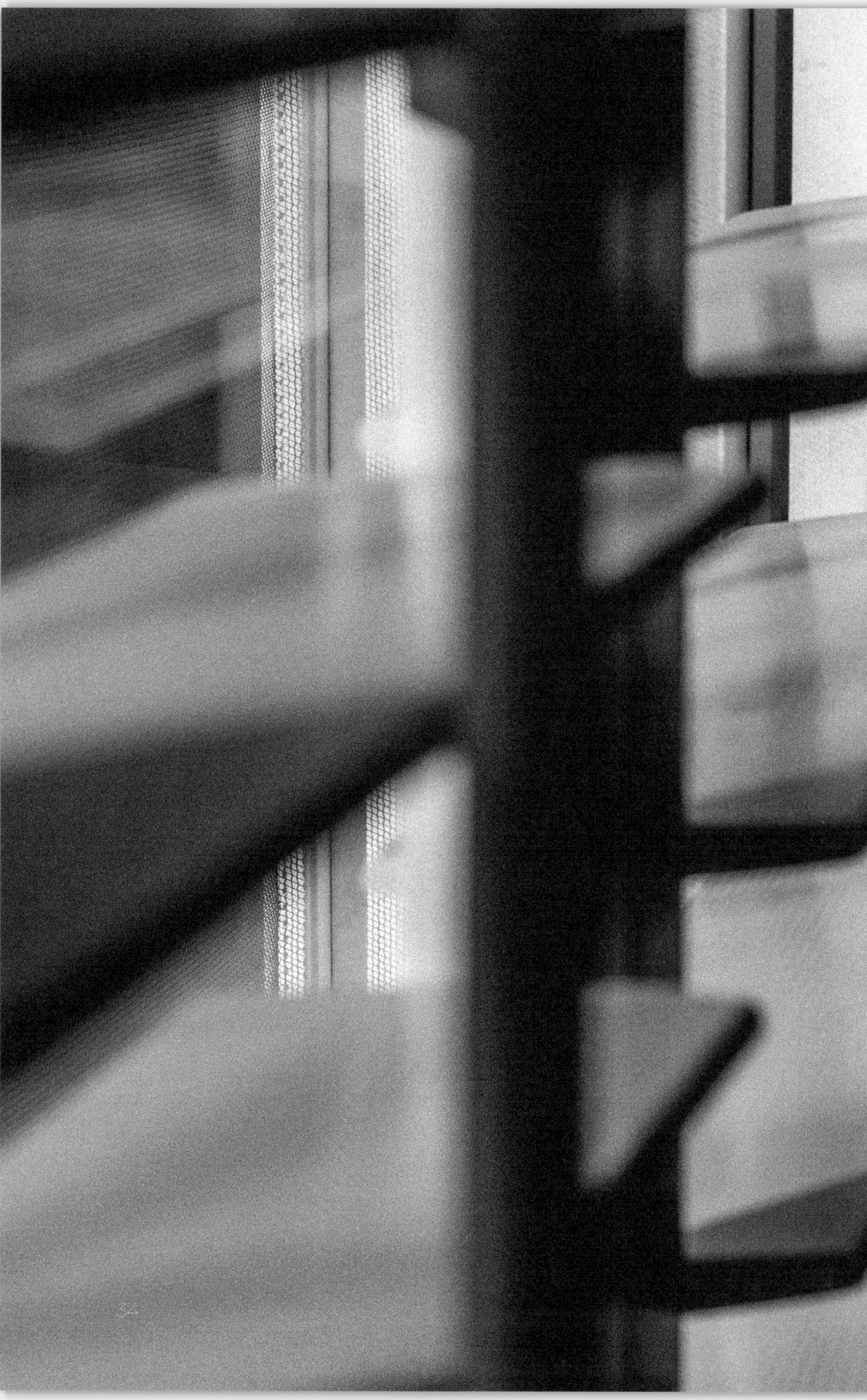

OVERGROWN

My window herb garden overflows with basil
And the cilantro I planted eight months ago.
I tied a rope to the sill to escape this,
But I'm afraid it might break,
I might scrape a knee on the adobe siding,
My hands are sure to slip.

It is 6 in the evening and
Hanna begs me to cook dinner,
We agreed on rice and chicken
Like yesterday and last week.
We talk of taking walks
Meeting the neighbors
Fixing our sleep schedules
Learning to play chess and calling our friends.
The sun sets into Denver's new curfew.

The overgrown oregano reminds me
I have not learned a new skill since February.
I reorganize the bookshelves
Every Saturday morning.
Pots and pans are sick of the same
Beans and eggs and unsalted potatoes.
I am no longer hungry for just food.

SUMMER ENDING

Desperately, we cling to the warm weather,
The sun run, light flood, big branches of summer.
Birds still prepare for flight.
Those of us waiting for a chill,
A sign from our brittle and shaking bones,
Have grown impatient.
Ignore the air getting lighter,
Ignore splitting lips and cracking knuckles.

I have now woken up exactly twice
Feeling the expectant cold of September.
There is a tumble of sheets that lie dormant on my bed
With knots and knots and fighting sleep.
Waking in a sweat is uncomfortable
    While the crisp of frost holds my flowers
    On the porch below me.

Something doesn't feel right
In the way my legs cross each other
The way that gourds don't mean autumn anymore.
Show me an escape to two years ago
When we yelled in the cornfield. It rained on our gaping mouths
And being lost in something of a child's game
    Wasn't so bad.

Now the dried up, nude cornstalks
Tell me that running will get me no further.
Tell me I have reached the center of the maze and
Not even the dirt caked under my heels can feed me.

My sweat-drenched sheets of corn-dreams will cold wash
And tumble dry. Right after I pulley my freight trained body from the window.

Today the light of dewy morning becomes less dewy
And dims to 57 degrees. But I get out of bed
To another 90 degree day,
Sweat perched on my lip,
And my knees swollen like waterlogged bricks.
They keep me down and force me to trudge
Through nothing but the last days of summer.

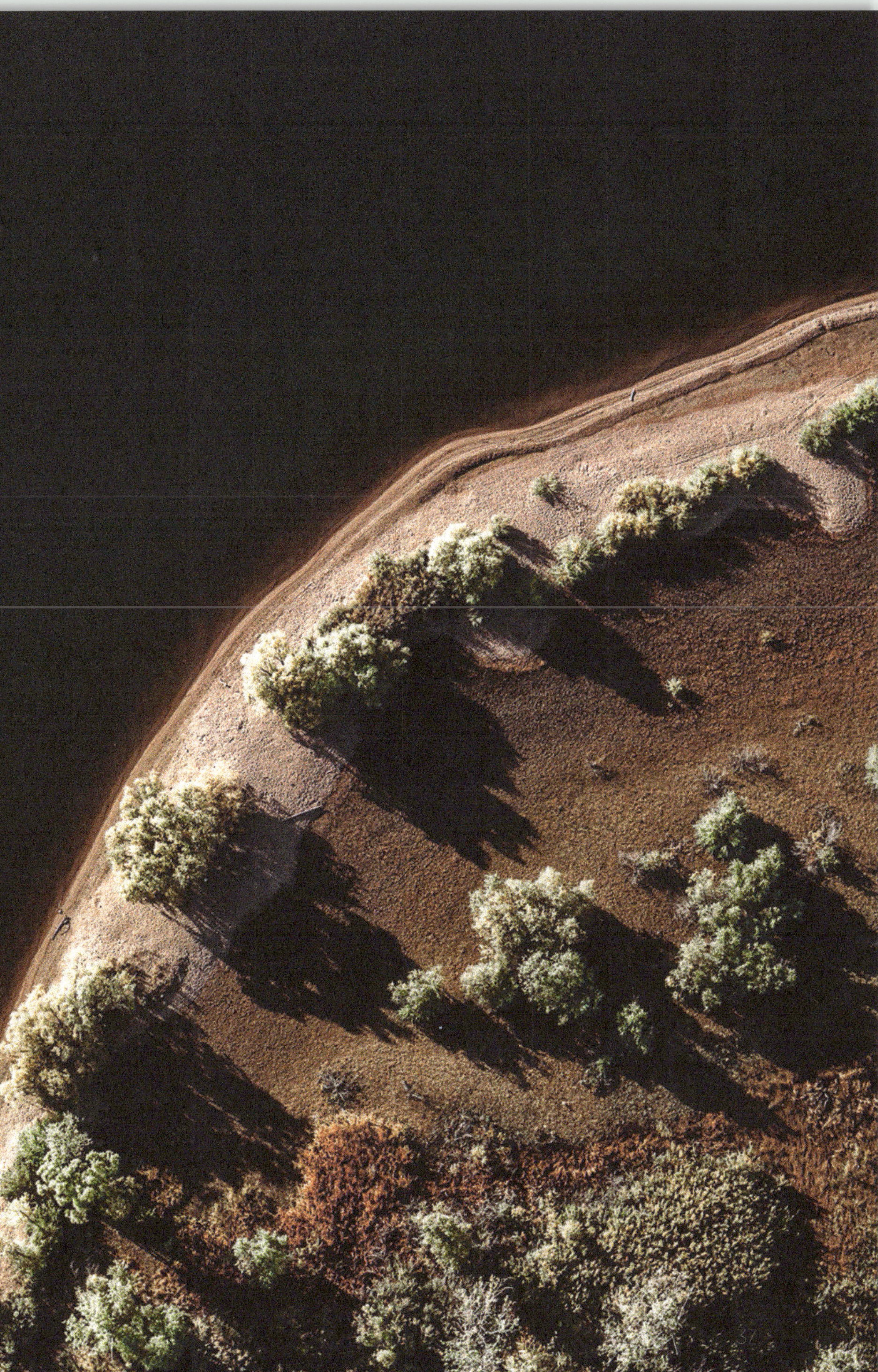

III

SUNBATHING ON THE PORCH AT 2:09 PM

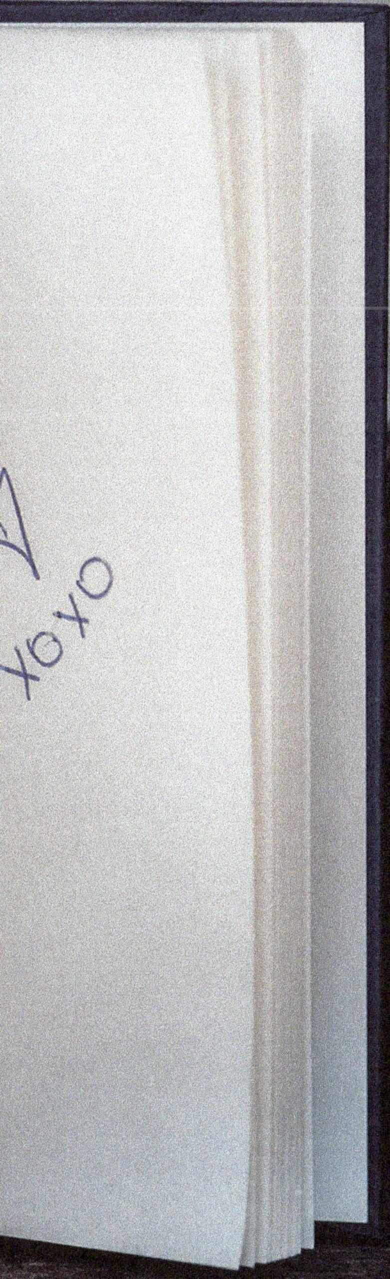

Paper is blinding in the sun
Like driving post-snow

Holding cardstock to the sunlight
I dream of shiny teardrops and watermarks,
An emotion I do not feel.
I am only bleached from the heat
And my arms become cold.

There are fingerprints on this postcard
That don't belong to me
But to another poet.
Prints familiar with expensive ink,
Black and blue finger pads.

I want to know the strangers across the street,
I want to know their porch-swing manicures
And window-frame eyelashes,
I want to turn their picket-fence sentences
Into verse, and mail a postcard to their doorstep.

BEECHWOOD

I am a mess of 10 trees
I am the essence nay
The aura of fine leaves.

I am the rouge of fall and
Vermillion sprinkles of reflection
In the pupils of lovers,
Of men who ask for daiquiris
And leave with bloody knuckles.

I am, in theory, dropping the decay
From my arms, leaves, if you may,
As they crush beneath passersby,
Under soon to be snow-trodden rain boots
And in time, I will be out of style.

Pieces of me will roam as browning corpses,
Clinging to muddy soles and wisps of wind.

The rest of me, a bare-boned,
Crisp-fanged remnant of earth,
Now waits for the 301st day of sun.

Naked sprig, bitter.
I am told I will last.

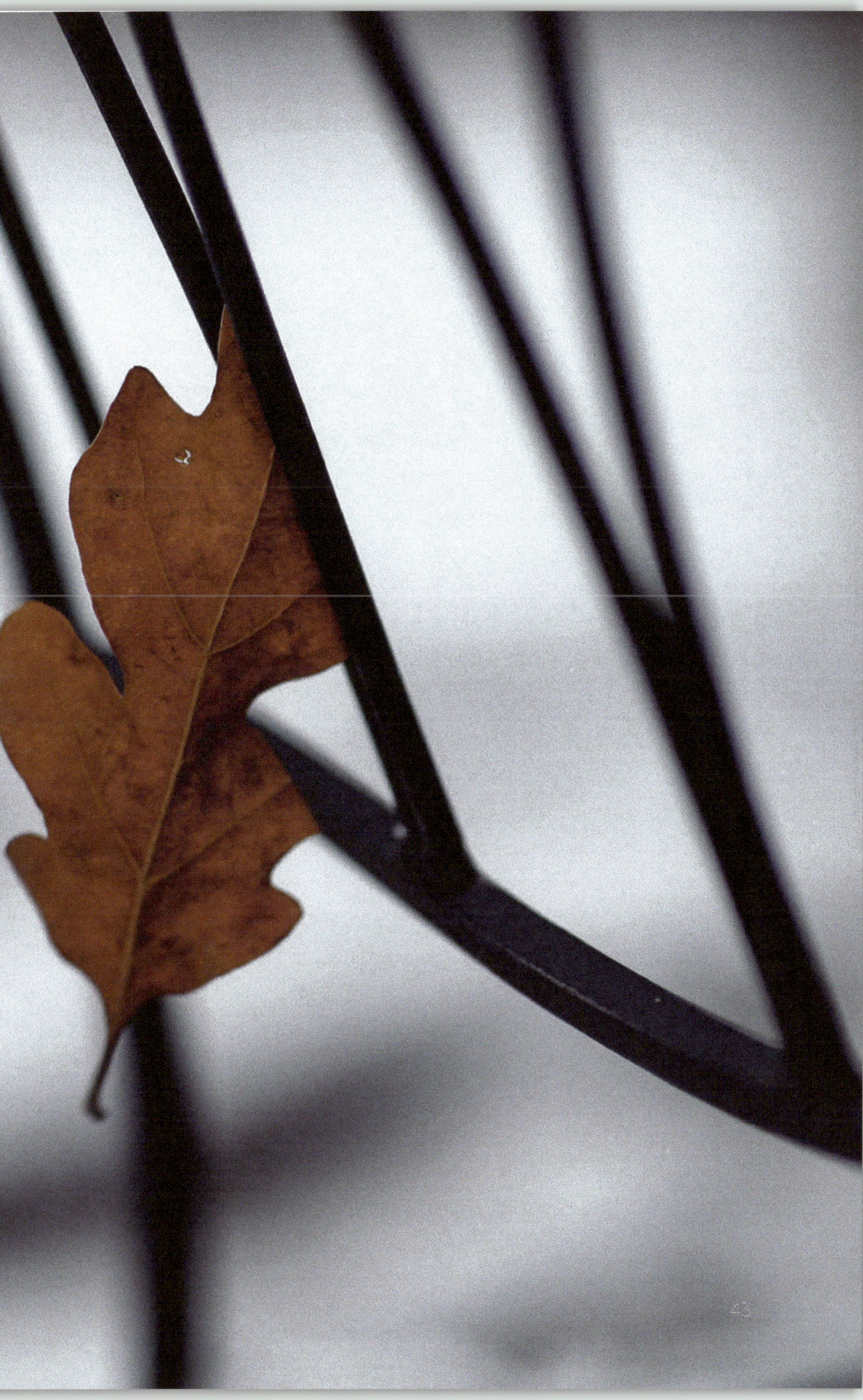

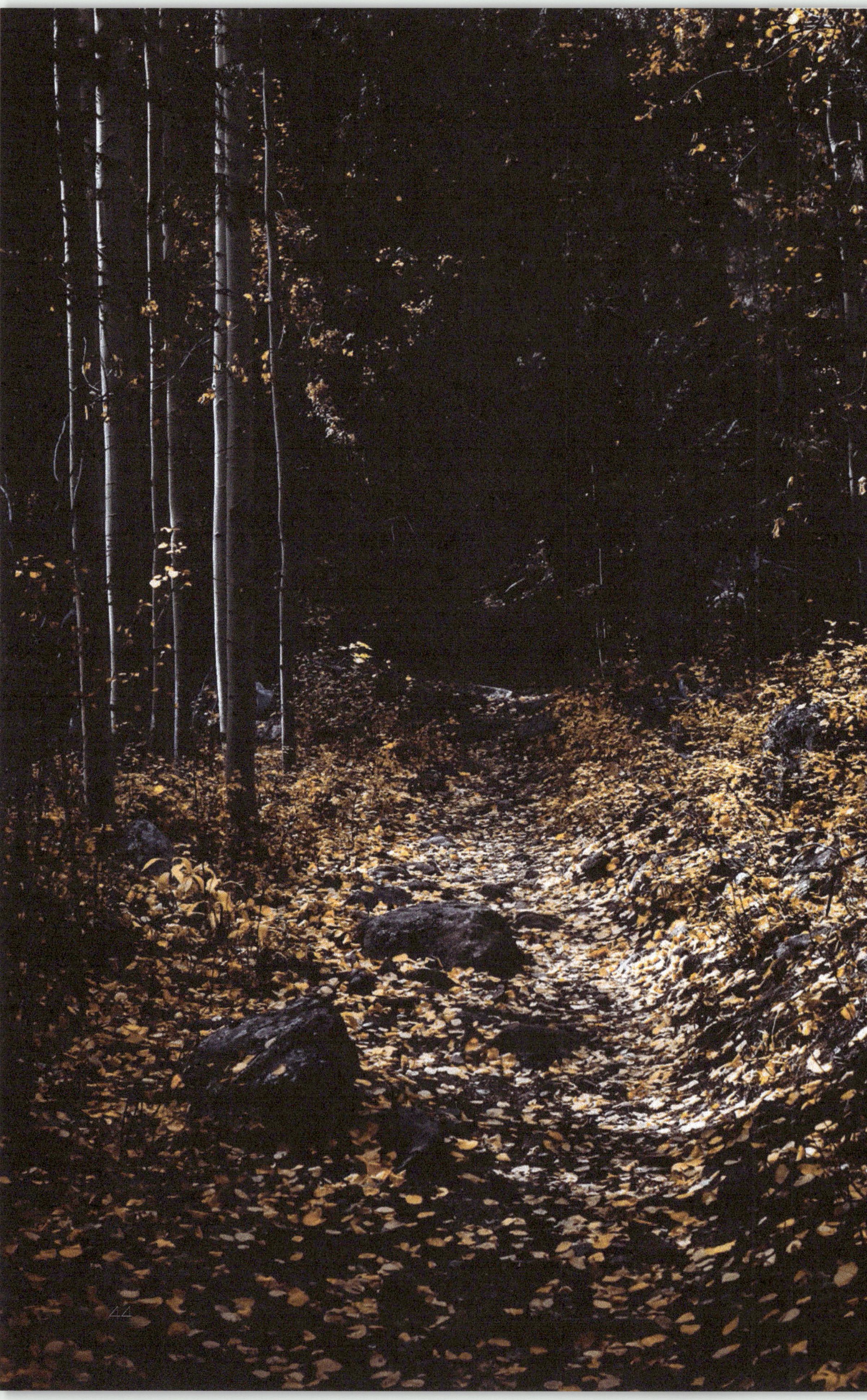

A CRISP MORNING SONNET

Fall. The season of decay. The sleepers
walk soundlessly from bedroom to bedroom.
Chills. On dying flower petals. Humming moon
and wind howls harmonize the hypnosis,
taking brittle aspen leaves down with it.
Burn. Decay can still burn yet it resumes
turning into cold stillness. Gold flakes. In ruin,
time will not offer a sort of stasis.
In night's chill, fire will not drown but rumble
mountains. Slow earth. Run away if I can
from fear. Into flawless, powdery thoughts.
Jump and jump and hang on. I cannot fall
if arms don't turn ill. Morning. I don't burn
as expected. The sun is no longer hot.

CURED

I see my grandmother
Watching recorded baseball games
And she asks if I watched the Rockies this Thursday;
A family ritual.

I see my parents walking to the store
Without hand sanitizer in their pockets.
Going on a light jog
Without breathing so heavily.

Tomorrow I will wake without pain,
Straighten my stature,
Unhinge my knees like a door
Swinging open and shut.

Sometimes I think the brown encrusted
Leaves of my garden will wear away
Or turn blush and lively again.

I've brewed peach ginger tea to help me sleep
And to make my stomach stop growling,
As if to put it all in motion.

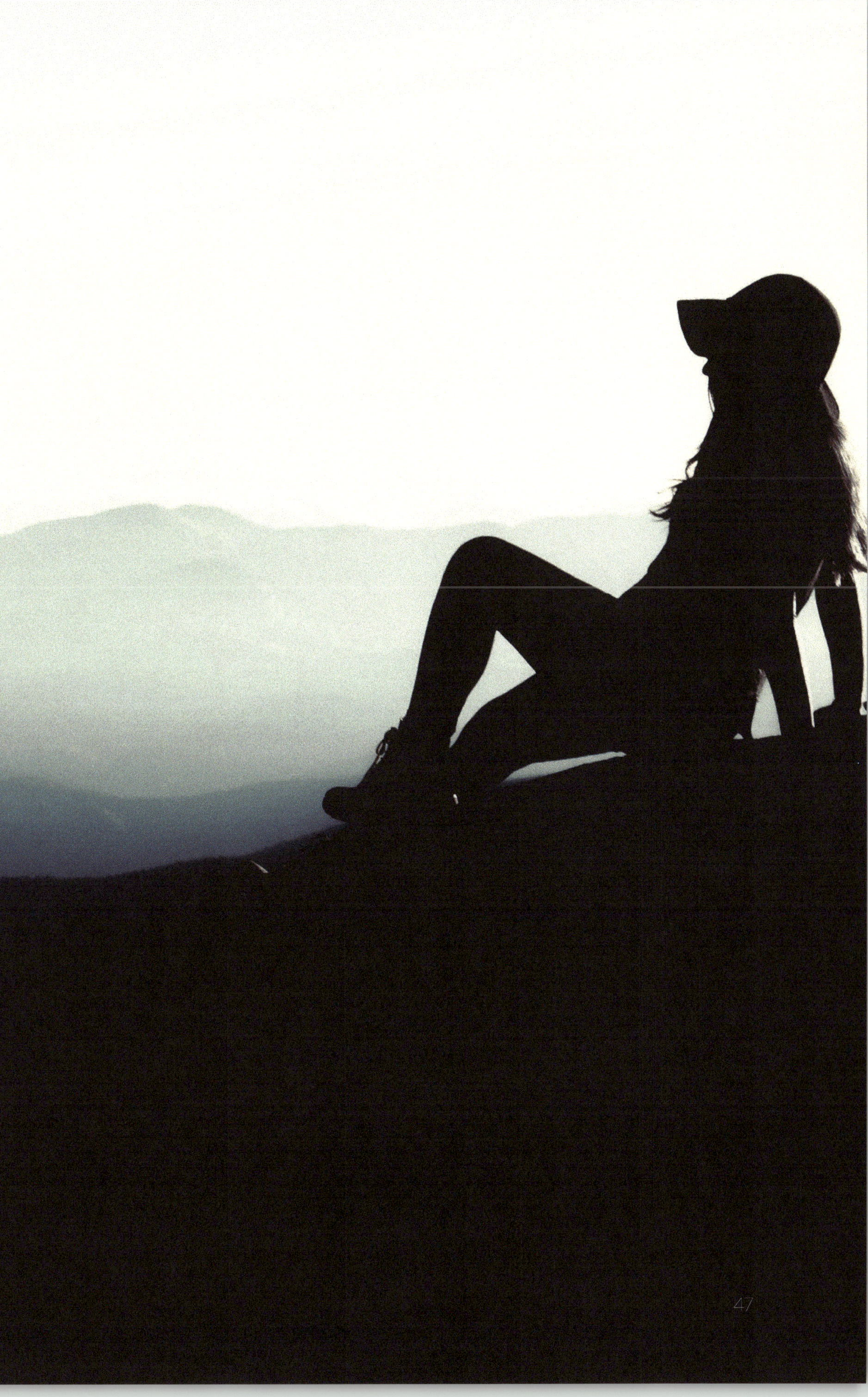

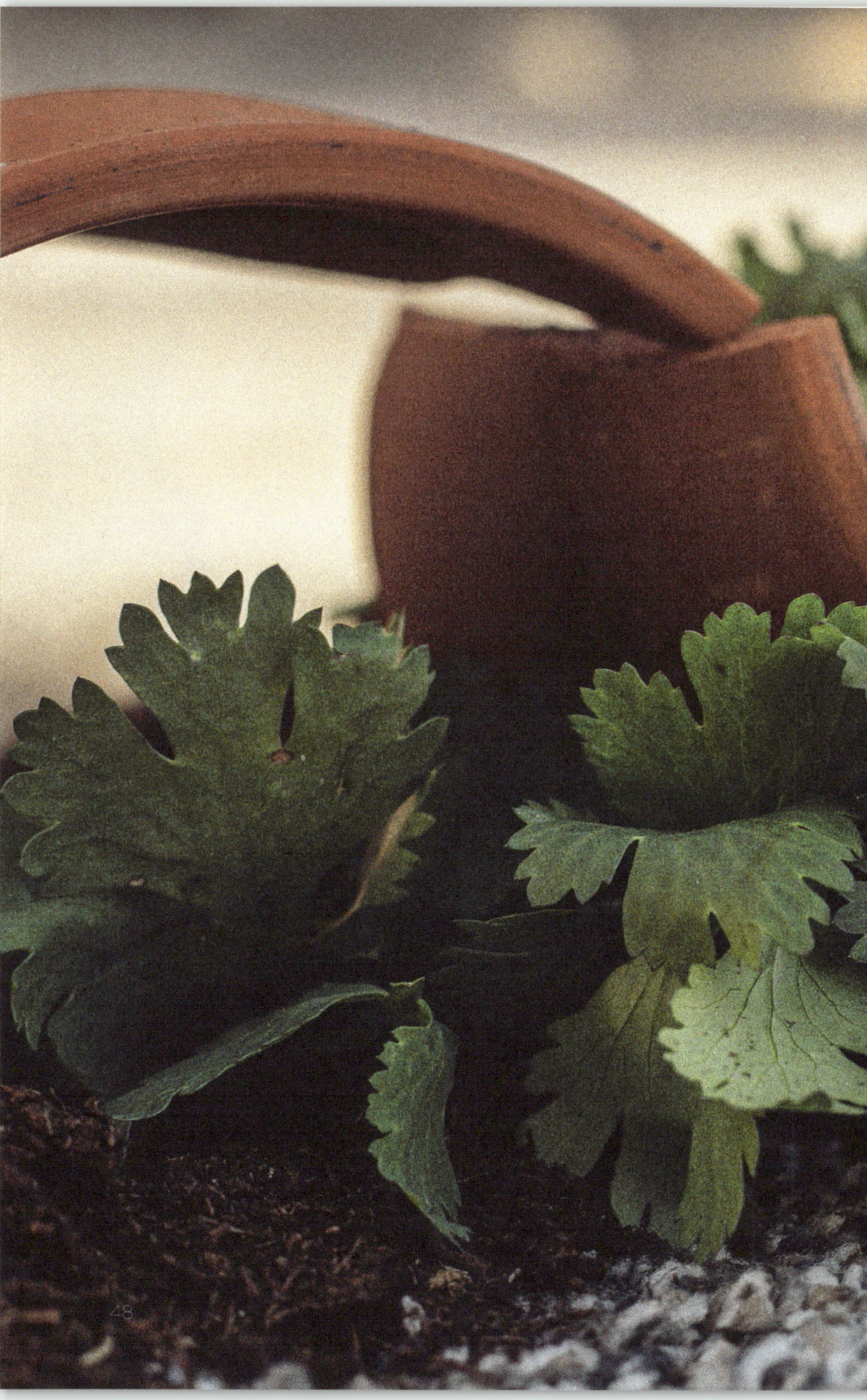

KNOCKED OVER

If I lie on the floor, the soil
Spilt from the pot wants to go back in.
Like a breeze or clawing vines
Could help collect the damp mess.
It's been eleven minutes since it tipped
And the terra cotta becomes dual-toned
Mildew and muddy
Rather than seeping its water into the carpet.

Imagine worms slinking back into the ground
Imagine the snag of torn leaves
Plucked leaves
Once buried, upturned.
Now the question to be upright.

There is a vibration in my cheek
Pressed into the cocoa-dusted floor;
Sod, top soil, too bitter for me.
A plate shift
A sandy fragment
And the pot will crack.
The stems look me in the eyes
Comfortably.

It's like rolling off the bed
Like tilted shelves and shattered picture frames
The 7am garbage truck
And a funeral.

A 2020 REEL

Today was a silent movie,
Individual and without a word
Waving without saying hello.
Happy. Outside.
Crossing the street again.
I felt less robotic than the plasma
Screen I watched all year.

My stony face and glazed eyes
Begin to crack in this movement.
Covered up, though, it becomes difficult
To see that you feel it too.

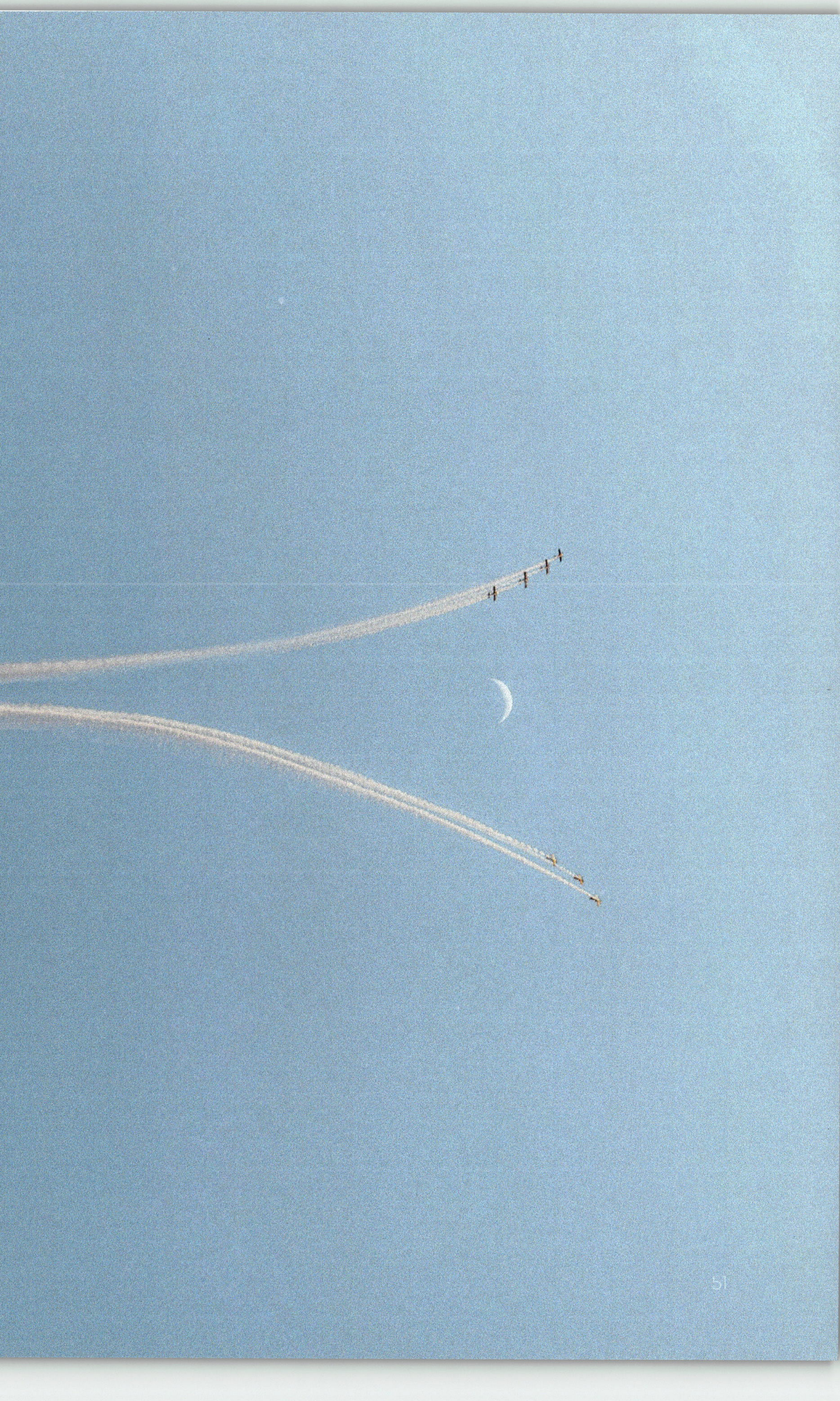

DEAR BRIAN

I've received your old book from
My mailman who does not know my name,
Probably does not know yours either.
I only know your name because it is written on the title page,
Where Sandra Lim wrote you a personal note
On October 21st, 2014,
That day you met her in Boston, apparently.

I was surprised to receive a signed, used copy
For only a few dollars and an Amazon account.
I am now one signature richer.
I asked Carl why he thinks you gave up a signed book
And he told me you must not have liked it.

I think you felt that someone else needed
To experience the book,
And only part of me worries something bad happened to you.

I hope you're well.
If you're looking for *The Wilderness*,
You know where to find it;
Only then I would let it go.

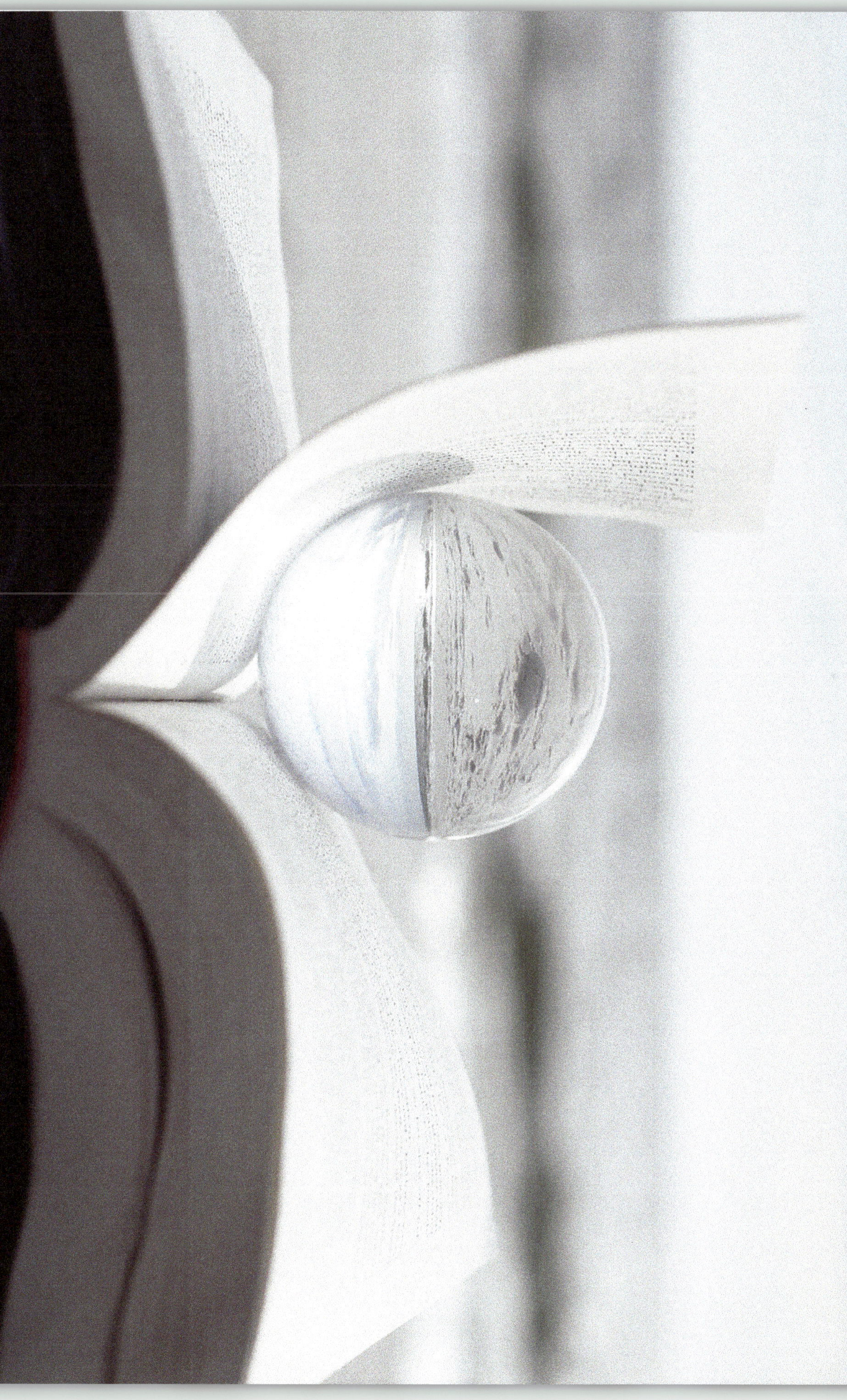

GRAY LUNGS

Remember Disney-themed Pez dispensers
And grandpa's old car in the garage
Always hidden under a tarp.
Imagine the haze of exhaust is like the wrinkles on his cheeks
And his smoky gray stubble.

Today is a fume. A hollow pipe of toxic breaths
Where the indoor air knocks me out cold.
Open a window please.
I cannot see what's next.
Light candles in my bedroom.

Look at this chandelier my mother once owned and
Its blue crystalline gem faces. I am a gem
But smudged; a fumed garage.
I'm still too young to really get it, though.

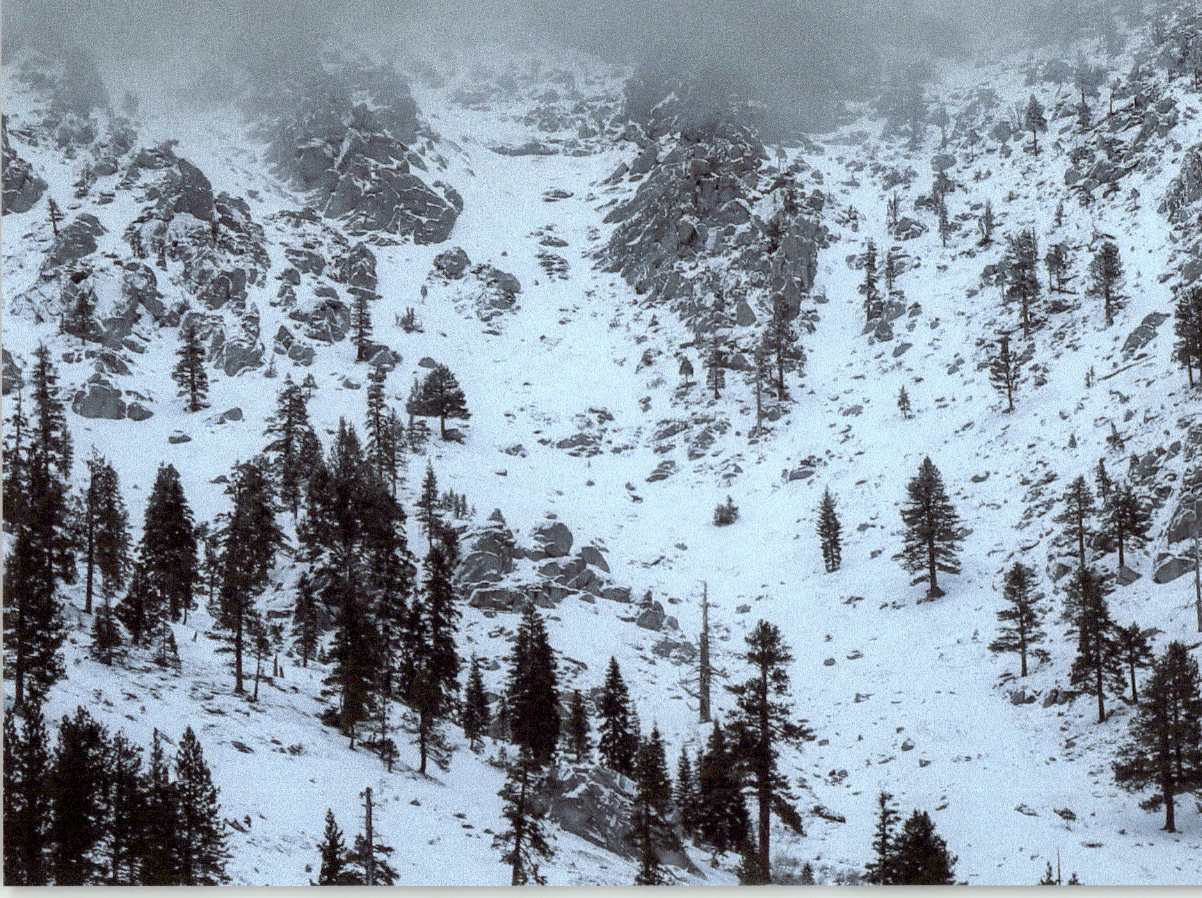

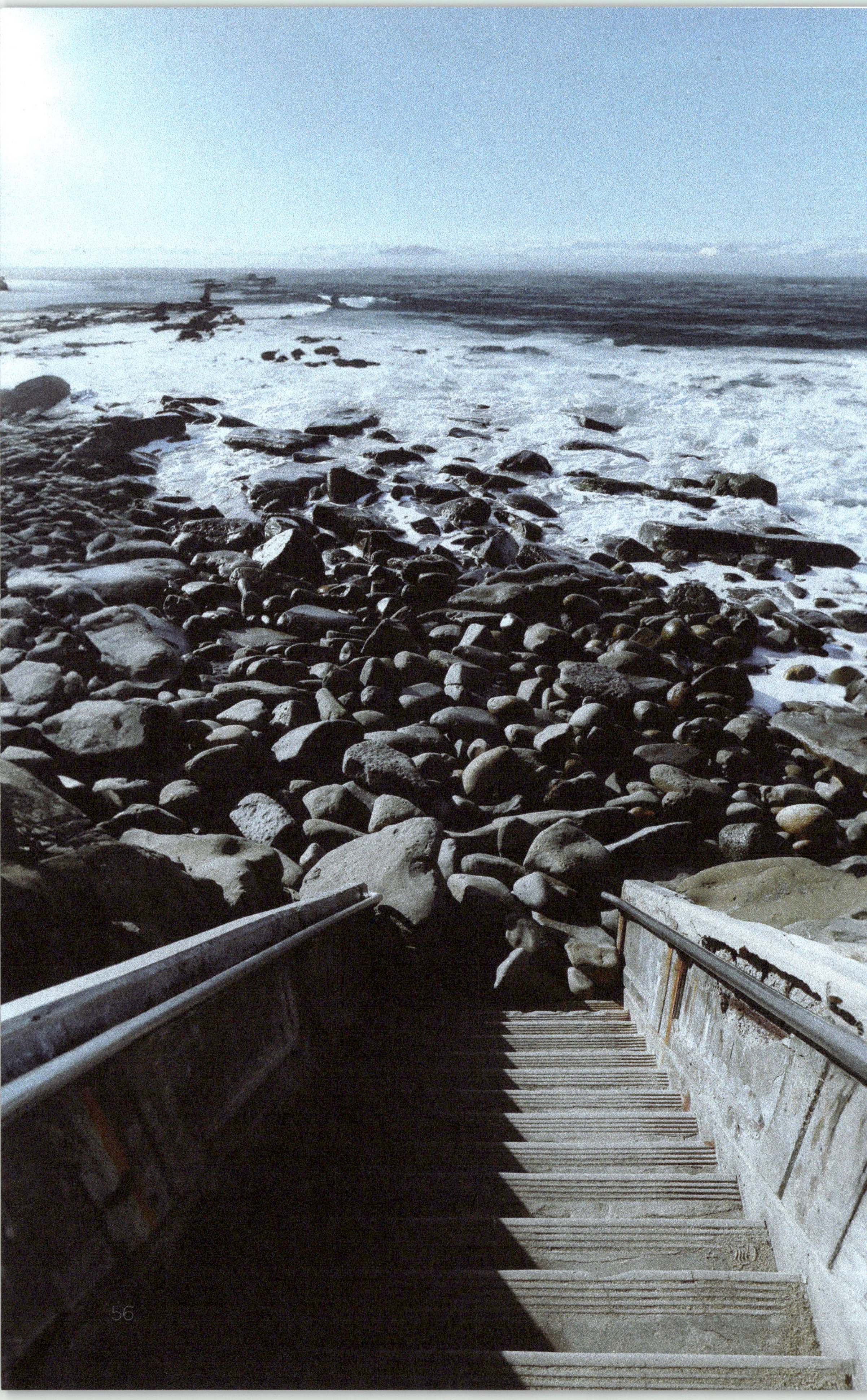

DYING ON THE STAIRS

I've been haunted
By the same idea for eight years,
That I can be a success
That I'll make it somewhere
By the end of the week.
Come May, come my freshly planted
Sunflowers in bloom,
They, too, will die where they began.

I think about the time
I planted two pots of flowers
To pass the days, but nothing happened.
It is again March.
It is again April.
When I lie down on the stairs my back still cracks.

There's a small painting in my bedroom
Of a staircase in a vast ocean, leading nowhere.
I think I walk these exact stairs each day
To the kitchen, to my bedroom,
Trying to grow sunflowers with the salt water.

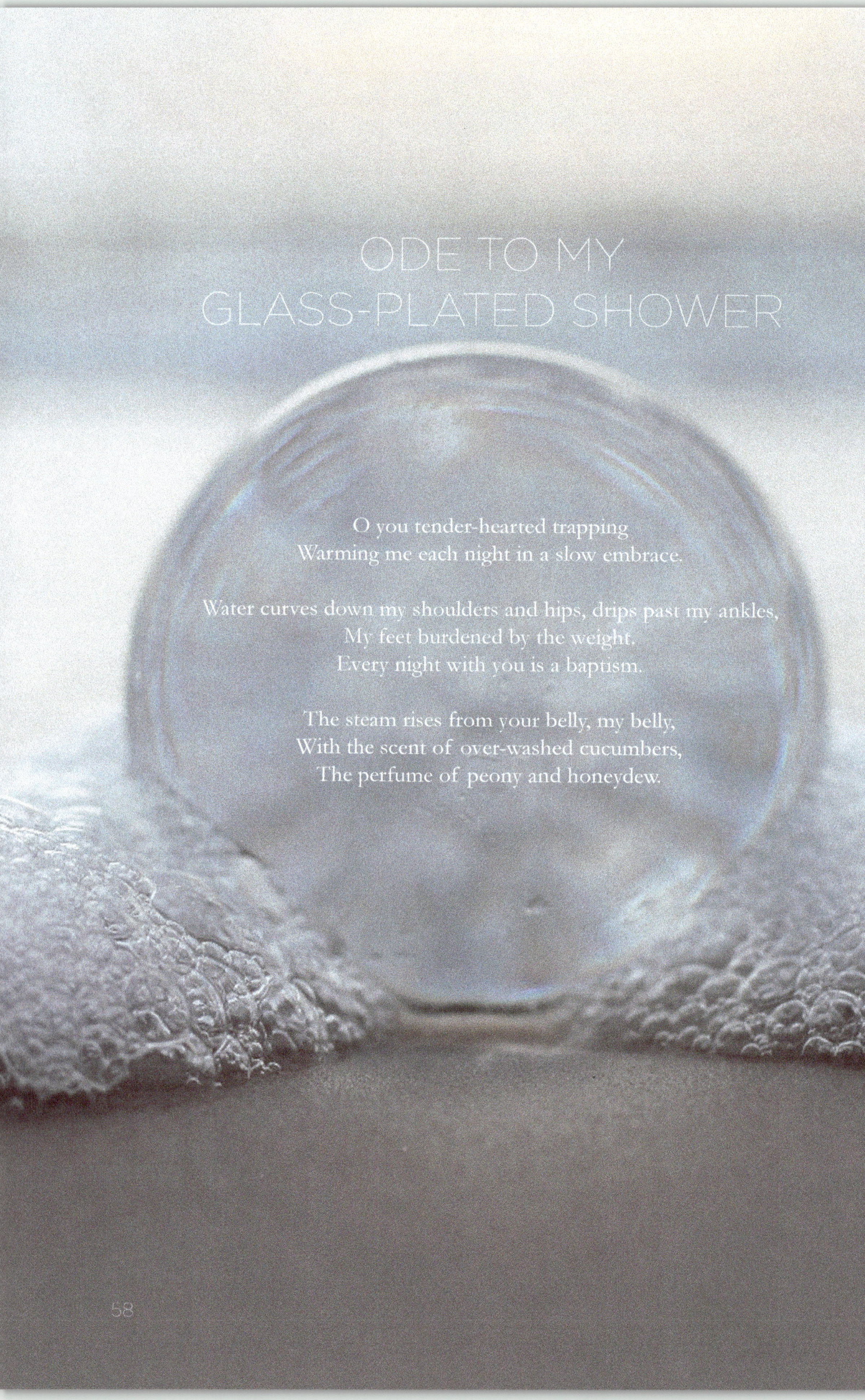

ODE TO MY GLASS-PLATED SHOWER

O you tender-hearted trapping
Warming me each night in a slow embrace.

Water curves down my shoulders and hips, drips past my ankles,
My feet burdened by the weight.
Every night with you is a baptism.

The steam rises from your belly, my belly,
With the scent of over-washed cucumbers,
The perfume of peony and honeydew.

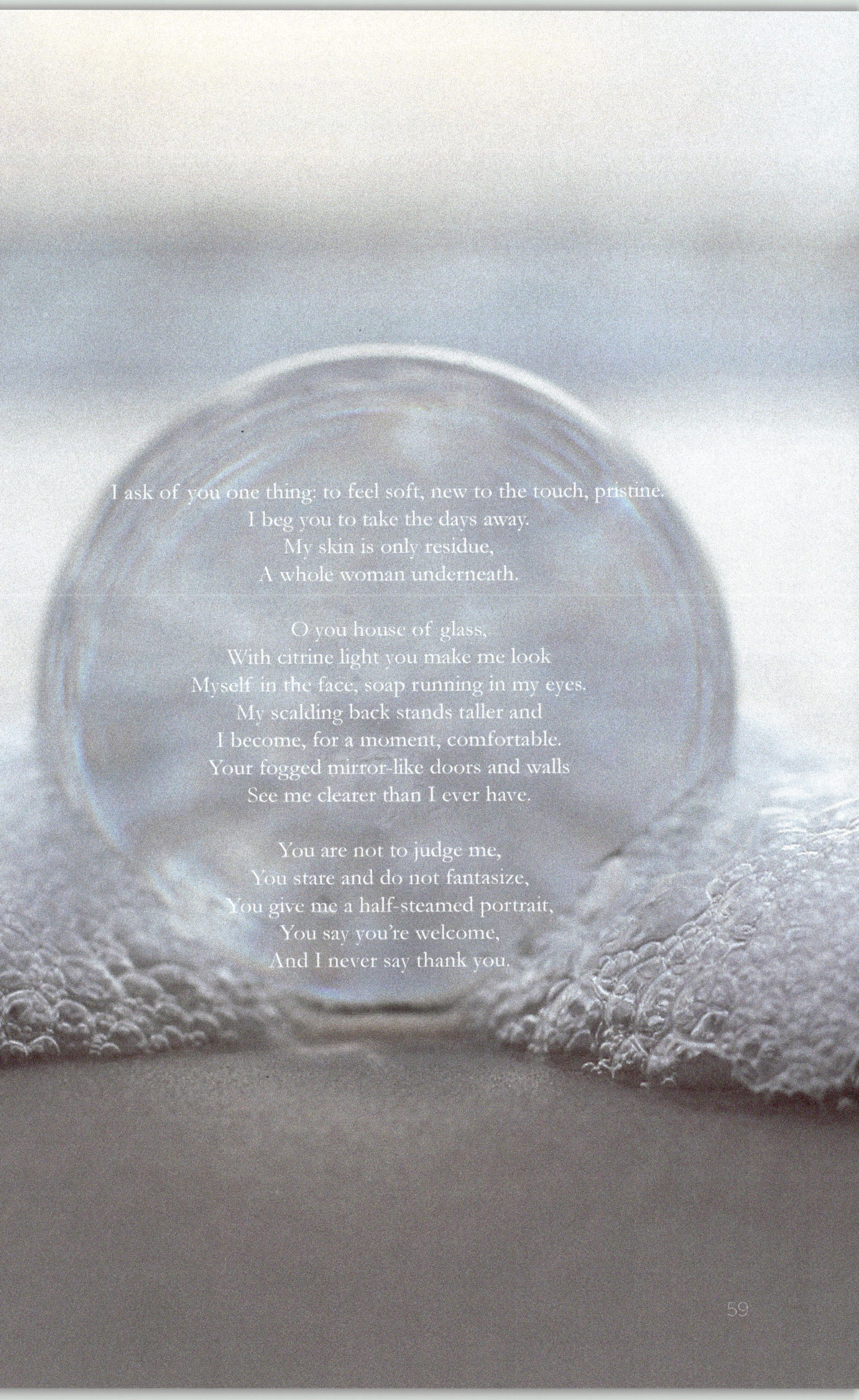

I ask of you one thing: to feel soft, new to the touch, pristine.
I beg you to take the days away.
My skin is only residue,
A whole woman underneath.

O you house of glass,
With citrine light you make me look
Myself in the face, soap running in my eyes.
My scalding back stands taller and
I become, for a moment, comfortable.
Your fogged mirror-like doors and walls
See me clearer than I ever have.

You are not to judge me,
You stare and do not fantasize,
You give me a half-steamed portrait,
You say you're welcome,
And I never say thank you.

ACKNOWLEDGEMENTS

I would like to thank *Cicada Creative Magazine*, *Foothills Magazine*, *Free the Verse*, and *Quagmire Literary Magazine* for publishing earlier versions of "Impression," "Something's Missing," "Strewn," "Knocked Over," and "Summer Ending" respectively. Thank you to Lindsay Turner, who gave me direction and reminded me to trust my writerly instincts. This work was crafted thanks to the opportunity to write a thesis for distinction at the University of Denver.

I would also like to thank my own network of editors and publishers who helped m along the way of self-publishing my debut book. From creating my own publishing house to getting every tedious legal detail correct, I would have been lost without Stacy Dymalski and the guidance of her book, *The Memoir Midwife: 9 Steps to Self-Publishing Your Own Book*. Stacy has always been a key mentor in the world of editing and she lent endless advice on how to get this book on the page and in people's hands. Likewise, Katie Mullaly of Surrogate Press was always just an email away for her best insight on the publishing process—especially when it came to heavy-duty color printing and hardcover requirements. Katie was this book's cheerleader from day one.

Finally, I want to thank my friends and family for nudging me along in the process. This book truly never would have seen the light of day—and certainly not in such a beautiful fashion—if it weren't for my sister, Missy Miller. It was Missy's idea to curate this book with both my poems and her photographs, and she was the driving force of this publication. What are sisters for, right?

ABOUT THE BOOK

his collection emerged from the quiet, uncertain days of the COVID-19 era. Callie's oems and Missy's photographs were created independently of one another, each apturing the emotions, moments, and memories of that time in distinct and ersonal ways.

he poems began as Callie's undergraduate thesis at the University of Denver. Vritten during the stillness of the pandemic, they explore introspection, quiet ndurance, and the emotional landscapes of a world on pause. Simultaneously, Missy hotographed her own experiences, capturing textures, spaces, and fleeting details hat, unbeknownst to her at the time, would later echo these poems' themes. When Missy later read Callie's poems for the first time, she discovered that her own hotographs strikingly mirrored the emotions of each work.

his debut book stands as both a testament to creativity in challenging times and a ecord of a pivotal period in life. It is a celebration of art, connection, and the rdinary beauty that endures.

ABOUT THE AUTHOR

Callie Miller is a poet and book editor based in Denver, Colorado. Her poetry has made appearances in both local and international publications, where her work has been recognized for its intimacy and attention to the subtle rhythms of everyday lif

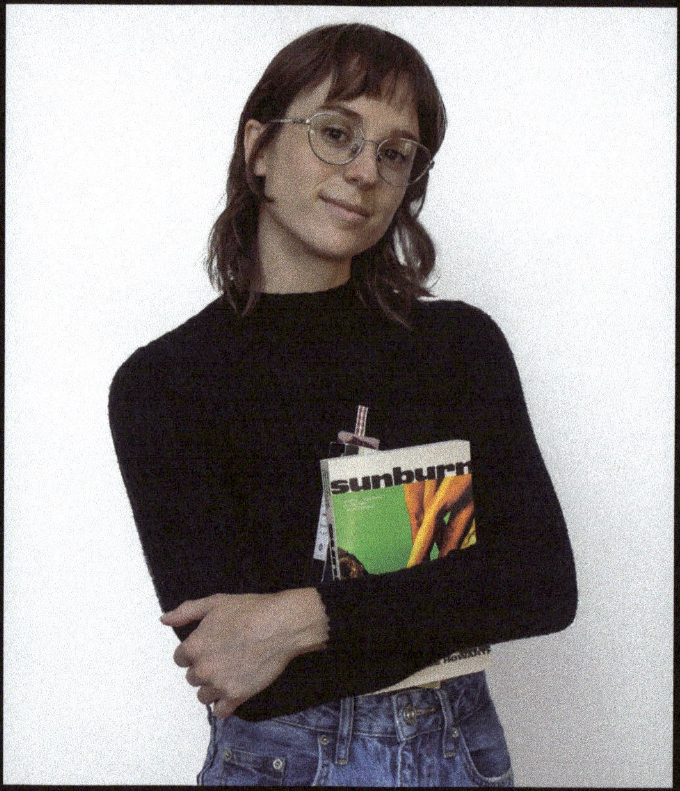

This debut collection bega as her undergraduate thesi at the University of Denver, earning her magn cum laude in 2021. These poems were written in the midst of the COVID-19 pandemic, a time that shaped her voice and themes as a poet within th quiet, stillness of the city. What started as an academ project grew into a body o work that explores resilience, loss, and the sm moments of beauty that carry us forward.

Beyond poetry, Callie has built a career in content writing and editing, with experience spanning corporate, nonprofit, and creative sectors. Whether working closely with clients or pursuing her own creative projects, she brings the same dedication to language: a belief in its power to connect, clarify, and create meaning.

This book is her first full-length publication, and she hopes it resonates with reader as profoundly as it did with her while writing it.

ABOUT THE PHOTOGRAPHER

Missy Miller is a photographer and media professional based in Denver, Colorado, currently living part-time in Northern Italy. She picked up a camera at twelve years old and has been documenting life ever since.

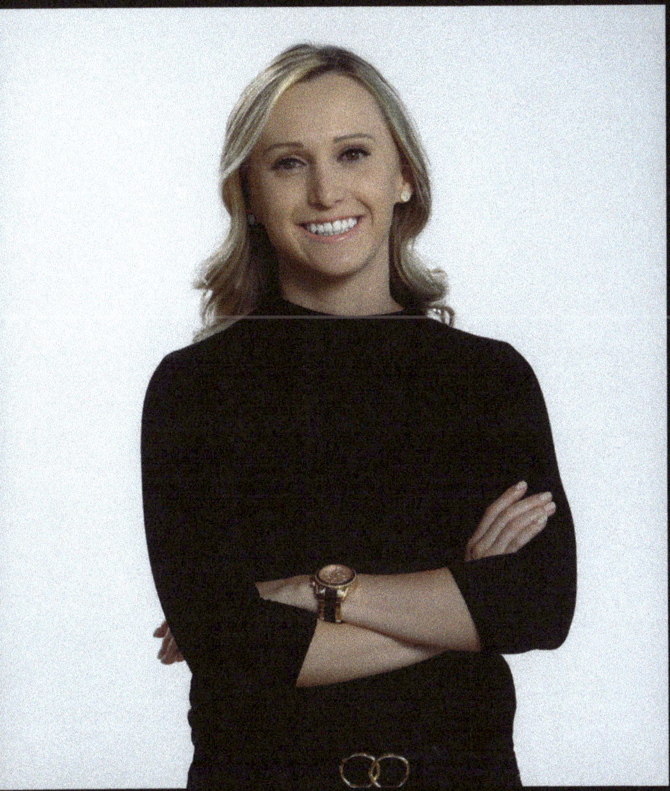

What began with photographing weddings and events through her high school and college years grew into the launch of her photography business, Moments by Missy LLC, in 2023. Her work reflects the connection between memory and place, capturing small, everyday moments that might otherwise be forgotten.

Alongside photography, Missy has built a career in social media marketing after earning her degree in Journalism and Media Communications with a minor in Leadership, Entrepreneurship, Arts, and Production from Colorado State University. She has worked with national sports organizations, global corporations, and now consults independently while pursuing her own creative projects and running her photography business.

This is her first book of published works.

www.ingramcontent.com/pod-product-compliance
Lightning Source LLC
LaVergne TN
LVHW070618110826
845155LV00009B/21